A PASSING GUEST

A
PASSING
GUEST

The story of a family through two centuries

STEPHANIE
MORGAN

SilverWood

Published by SilverWood Books 2012
www.silverwoodbooks.co.uk

ISBN 978-1-906236-98-4

British Library Cataloguing in Publication Data
A CIP catalogue record for this book is available from the British Library

Set in Sabon by SilverWood Books
Printed on responsibly sourced paper

I dedicate this book to my children,
Nicholas, Charlotte and Simon, and to my grandchildren,
Caroline and Christopher Morgan, James, Lucy
and Tom Maizels and Anna and Jack Morgan, with love

I am a passing guest, as all our fathers were
Psalm 39:12

Contents

Preface

When I began to write this book – and it has taken me over four years – I had an imagined great-grandchild in mind as one of the future readers, and to him or her I send warm greetings. What you will be like I will never know. Your life experience is likely to be as different from mine as mine has been from my forebears. I hope, however, that you will find the story of my (and therefore your) family as enthralling as I found that of my great-grandfather and other ancestors.

Can we be 'proud' of our lineage? After all, we have done absolutely nothing to deserve it, having simply had the good fortune to be born into a certain clan, the past generations of which appear to have lived by a set of standards that enabled them to contribute much to previous times and to enhance a good deal of the nineteenth, all of the twentieth and the beginning of the twenty-first centuries. They passed on more than their genes and there is much to be learnt from them.

They have been, on the whole, very family-minded, enjoying tribal gatherings, keeping in touch with each other and rallying with timely help to those needing it. The mechanism of news-distribution is remarkably well oiled. The support that this engenders is extremely valuable.

They have worked hard at their chosen professions

and some have risen in the world. They have mostly stayed married to the spouse they first chose and have been loving and supportive of their children. Many have fought for their country and some have died for the same cause. They seem to have inherited an exhilarating and vigorous sense of humour, without which life can be tedious.

Have I made them sound too perfect, like the smiling ideal family in a 1950s advertisement for Oxo cubes? There are probably a few black or grey sheep lurking among the white – human beings, after all, tend not to be altogether faultless – but the fact is that I can't at the moment name one – and might think twice before doing so anyway. Mostly they have been good, solid citizens lightening their useful lives with wit, mutual affection and much laughter.

By the time that you are as old as I am now I hope (one can always *hope*) that wars will have become things of the past, that less inequality will exist between people and between nations, that more cures have been found for horrible diseases and that global warming hasn't made life on Earth too uncomfortable. It is to be hoped that you will not have to contemplate abandoning the Earth for another planet. All being well, I wish you a happy and fulfilled life.

The story of my father's grandfather is an alluring and unexpected glimpse into another age. I have discovered some almost equally beguiling anecdotes of other forebears, among them three Morgan brothers who, respectively, became a President of the Law Society, a Bishop and an Admiral. Enterprising clergymen by the dozen, teachers, seamen and soldiers, Colonial Officers and architects, writers and farmers, travellers and doctors, publishers and bankers, nuns and missionaries – ordinary folk leading practical and constructive lives, are among those who fill many slots in the family trees of Rosedales, Morgans, Pellys, Edmonds and related kin – and of you, dear descendant.

So, 'On We Go' – as Morgans are apt to say – into whatever comes next in the world. Not having been supplied with crystal balls, we who are around at present can only speculate as to what this might be, but you, when it comes to your turn, will use your inherited energy, intelligence, compassion, spirit of adventure and sense of humour to cope with it. Perhaps you will write your own memoir to keep the family history up to date.

I have been helped and encouraged to write this book in many ways and by numerous people. I discovered, by a stroke of luck, the one remaining place on the 'Write Now' course in Petersfield in 2007 when I had just begun this memoir. For the next three years there followed a life-changing series of eight-week winter evening gatherings when we students were instructed, cajoled, even bullied in the mildest way, into the art of writing, by our two inspirational tutors, Russell Twisk and Colin Dunne, distinguished writers both. My gratitude to them is immense.

Sheila Dainton, the administrator, organised the courses, found the venues, provided life-saving tea and biscuits, and wrote, as a fellow student, humorously and beautifully. (She also supplied some much-needed grammatical and other advice for this book.) Not only did we all laugh a good deal of the time, but we made progress in our chosen subject and, much more importantly, truly lasting friendships.

I am also very grateful to my daughter-in-law, Sally Morgan, for her technical help in sorting out the family trees and to my grandson, Christopher, for his expertise with images.

Rosedale Family Tree

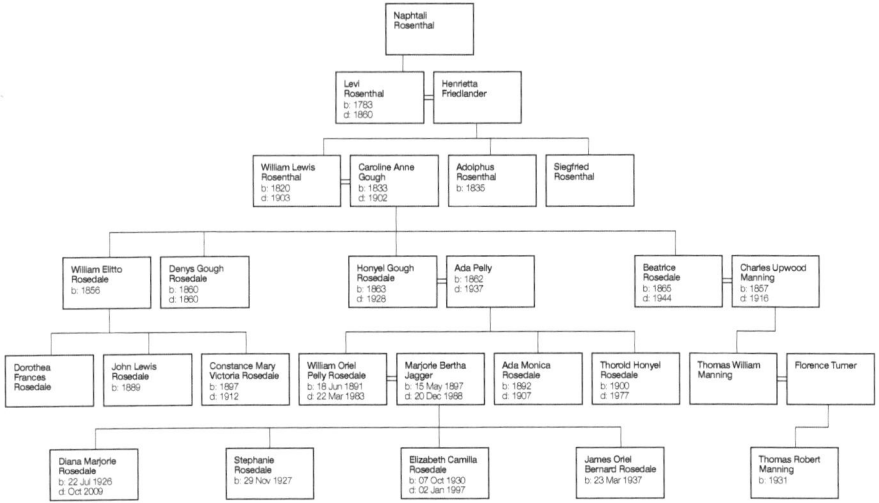

Naphtali Rosenthal

Levi Rosenthal
b: 1783
d: 1860

Henrietta Friedlander

William Lewis Rosenthal
b: 1820
d: 1903

Caroline Anne Gough
b: 1833
d: 1902

Adolphus Rosenthal
b: 1835

Siegfried Rosenthal

William Elitto Rosedale
b: 1856

Denys Gough Rosedale
b: 1860
d: 1860

Honyel Gough Rosedale
b: 1863
d: 1926

Ada Pelly
b: 1862
d: 1937

Beatrice Rosedale
b: 1865
d: 1944

Charles Upwood Manning
b: 1857
d: 1916

Dorothea Frances Rosedale

John Lewis Rosedale
b: 1889

Constance Mary Victoria Rosedale
b: 1897
d: 1912

William Oriel Pelly Rosedale
b: 18 Jun 1891
d: 22 Mar 1983

Marjorie Bertha Jagger
b: 15 May 1897
d: 20 Dec 1988

Ada Monica Rosedale
b: 1892
d: 1907

Thorold Honyel Rosedale
b: 1900
d: 1977

Thomas William Manning

Florence Turner

Diana Marjorie Rosedale
b: 22 Jul 1926
d: Oct 2009

Stephanie Rosedale
b: 29 Nov 1927

Elizabeth Camilla Rosedale
b: 07 Oct 1930
d: 02 Jan 1997

James Oriel Bernard Rosedale
b: 23 Mar 1937

Thomas Robert Manning
b: 1931

Diana's Family Tree

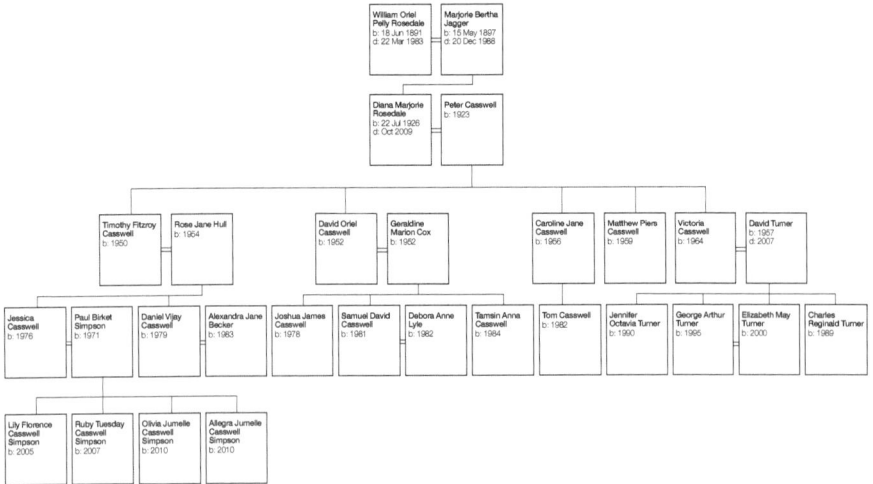

William Oriel Pelly Rosedale
b: 18 Jun 1891
d: 22 Mar 1983

Marjorie Bertha Jagger
b: 15 May 1897
d: 20 Dec 1988

Diana Marjorie Rosedale
b: 22 Jul 1926
d: Oct 2009

Peter Casswell
b: 1923

Timothy Fitzroy Casswell
b: 1950

Rose Jane Hull
b: 1954

David Oriel Casswell
b: 1952

Geraldine Marion Cox
b: 1952

Caroline Jane Casswell
b: 1956

Matthew Piers Casswell
b: 1959

Victoria Casswell
b: 1964

David Turner
b: 1957
d: 2007

Jessica Casswell
b: 1976

Paul Birket Simpson
b: 1971

Daniel Vijay Casswell
b: 1979

Alexandra Jane Becker
b: 1983

Joshua James Casswell
b: 1978

Samuel David Casswell
b: 1981

Debora Anne Lyle
b: 1982

Tamsin Anna Casswell
b: 1984

Tom Casswell
b: 1982

Jennifer Octavia Turner
b: 1990

George Arthur Turner
b: 1995

Elizabeth May Turner
b: 2000

Charles Reginald Turner
b: 1989

Lily Florence Casswell Simpson
b: 2005

Ruby Tuesday Casswell Simpson
b: 2007

Olivia Jumelle Casswell Simpson
b: 2010

Allegra Jumelle Casswell Simpson
b: 2010

Stephanie's Family Tree

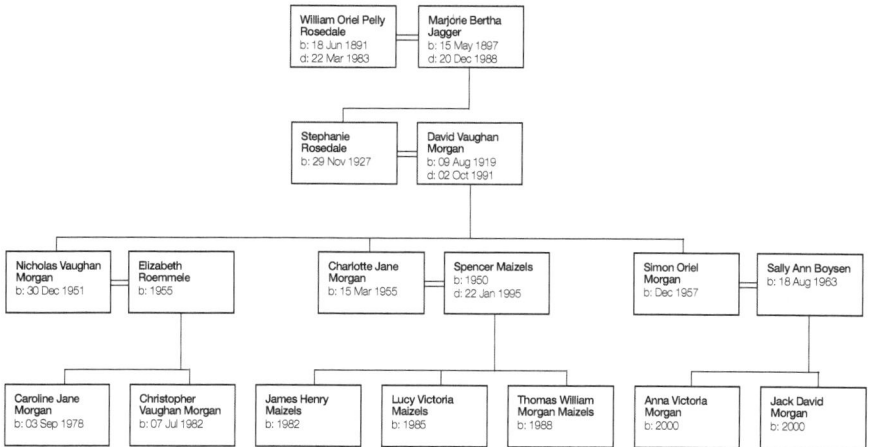

```
William Oriel Pelly          Marjorie Bertha
Rosedale                     Jagger
b: 18 Jun 1891               b: 15 May 1897
d: 22 Mar 1983               d: 20 Dec 1988
```

```
Stephanie                    David Vaughan
Rosedale                     Morgan
b: 29 Nov 1927               b: 09 Aug 1919
                             d: 02 Oct 1991
```

```
Nicholas Vaughan   Elizabeth        Charlotte Jane    Spencer Maizels      Simon Oriel      Sally Ann Boysen
Morgan             Roemmele         Morgan            b: 1950              Morgan           b: 18 Aug 1963
b: 30 Dec 1951     b: 1955          b: 15 Mar 1955    d: 22 Jan 1995       b: Dec 1957
```

```
Caroline Jane      Christopher      James Henry      Lucy Victoria    Thomas William       Anna Victoria    Jack David
Morgan             Vaughan Morgan   Maizels          Maizels          Morgan Maizels       Morgan           Morgan
b: 03 Sep 1978     b: 07 Jul 1982   b: 1982          b: 1985          b: 1988              b: 2000          b: 2000
```

Camilla's Family Tree

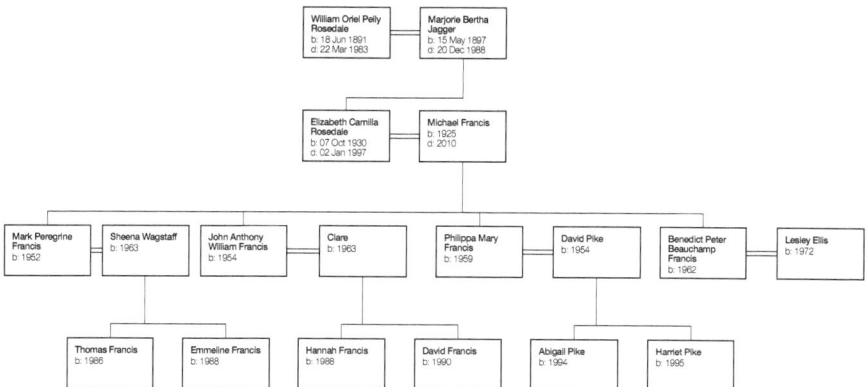

```
William Oriel Pelly          Marjorie Bertha
Rosedale                     Jagger
b: 18 Jun 1891               b: 15 May 1897
d: 22 Mar 1983               d: 20 Dec 1988
```

```
Elizabeth Camilla            Michael Francis
Rosedale                     b: 1925
b: 07 Oct 1930               d: 2010
d: 02 Jan 1997
```

```
Mark Peregrine   Sheena Wagstaff   John Anthony    Clare        Philippa Mary   David Pike    Benedict Peter    Lesley Ellis
Francis          b: 1963           William Francis b: 1963      Francis         b: 1954       Beauchamp         b: 1972
b: 1952                            b: 1954                      b: 1959                       Francis
                                                                                             b: 1962
```

```
Thomas Francis   Emmeline Francis   Hannah Francis   David Francis    Abigail Pike     Harriet Pike
b: 1986          b: 1988            b: 1988          b: 1990          b: 1994          b: 1995
```

Barney's Family Tree

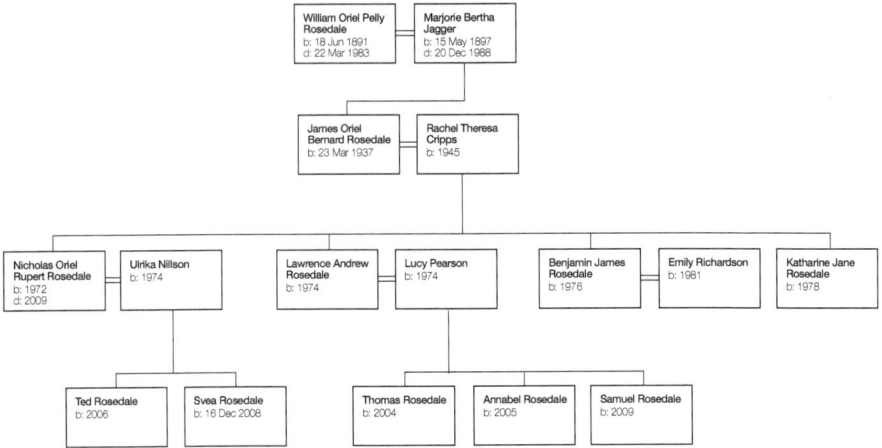

- William Oriel Pelly Rosedale
  b: 18 Jun 1891
  d: 22 Mar 1983
- Marjorie Bertha Jagger
  b: 15 May 1897
  d: 20 Dec 1988

- James Oriel Bernard Rosedale
  b: 23 Mar 1937
- Rachel Theresa Cripps
  b: 1945

- Nicholas Oriel Rupert Rosedale
  b: 1972
  d: 2009
- Ulrika Nillson
  b: 1974
- Lawrence Andrew Rosedale
  b: 1974
- Lucy Pearson
  b: 1974
- Benjamin James Rosedale
  b: 1976
- Emily Richardson
  b: 1981
- Katharine Jane Rosedale
  b: 1978

- Ted Rosedale
  b: 2006
- Svea Rosedale
  b: 16 Dec 2008
- Thomas Rosedale
  b: 2004
- Annabel Rosedale
  b: 2005
- Samuel Rosedale
  b: 2009

Pelly Family Tree

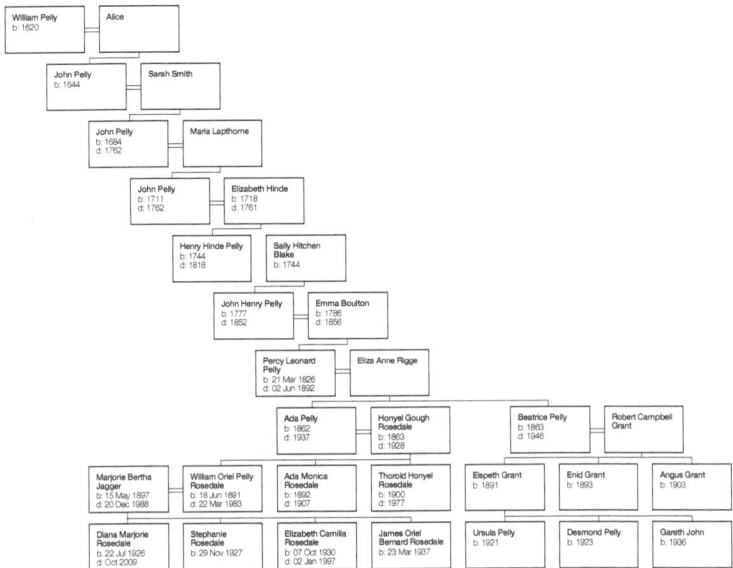

- William Pelly
  b: 1620
- Alice

- John Pelly
  b: 1644
- Sarah Smith

- John Pelly
  b: 1684
  d: 1762
- Maria Lapthorne

- John Pelly
  b: 1711
  d: 1762
- Elizabeth Hinde
  b: 1718
  d: 1761

- Henry Hinde Pelly
  b: 1744
  d: 1818
- Sally Hitchen Blake
  b: 1744

- John Henry Pelly
  b: 1777
  d: 1852
- Emma Boulton
  b: 1796
  d: 1856

- Percy Leonard Pelly
  b: 21 Mar 1826
  d: 02 Jun 1892
- Eliza Anne Rigge

- Ada Pelly
  b: 1862
  d: 1937
- Honyel Gough Rosedale
  b: 1863
  d: 1928
- Beatrice Pelly
  b: 1863
  d: 1946
- Robert Campbell Grant

- Marjorie Bertha Jagger
  b: 15 May 1897
  d: 20 Dec 1988
- William Oriel Pelly Rosedale
  b: 18 Jun 1891
  d: 22 Mar 1983
- Ada Monica Rosedale
  b: 1892
  d: 1907
- Thorold Honyel Rosedale
  b: 1900
  d: 1977
- Elspeth Grant
  b: 1891
- Enid Grant
  b: 1893
- Angus Grant
  b: 1903

- Diana Marjorie Rosedale
  b: 22 Jul 1926
  d: Oct 2009
- Stephanie Rosedale
  b: 29 Nov 1927
- Elizabeth Camilla Rosedale
  b: 07 Oct 1930
  d: 02 Jan 1997
- James Oriel Bernard Rosedale
  b: 23 Mar 1937
- Ursula Pelly
  b: 1921
- Desmond Pelly
  b: 1923
- Gareth John
  b: 1936

Theophilus Morgan to Joseph John Morgan

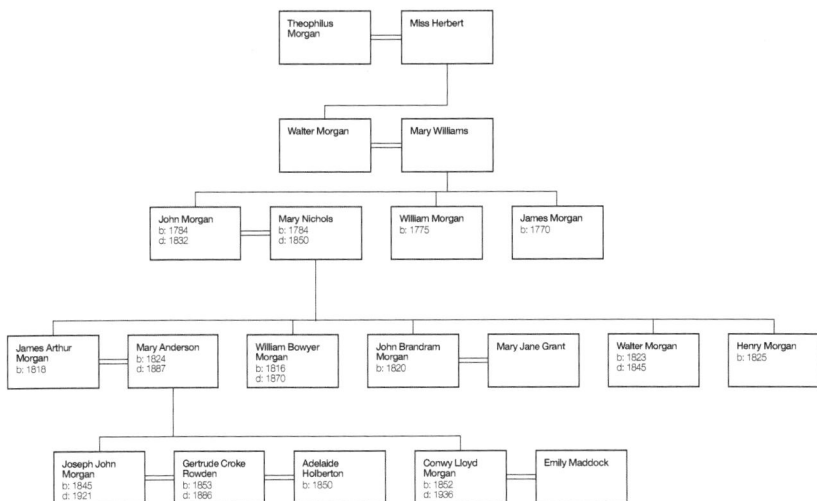

- Theophilus Morgan
- Miss Herbert

- Walter Morgan
- Mary Williams

- John Morgan
  b: 1784
  d: 1832
- Mary Nichols
  b: 1784
  d: 1850
- William Morgan
  b: 1775
- James Morgan
  b: 1770

- James Arthur Morgan
  b: 1818
- Mary Anderson
  b: 1824
  d: 1887
- William Bowyer Morgan
  b: 1816
  d: 1870
- John Brandram Morgan
  b: 1820
- Mary Jane Grant
- Walter Morgan
  b: 1823
  d: 1845
- Henry Morgan
  b: 1825

- Joseph John Morgan
  b: 1845
  d: 1921
- Gertrude Croke Rowden
  b: 1853
  d: 1886
- Adelaide Holberton
  b: 1850
- Conwy Lloyd Morgan
  b: 1852
  d: 1936
- Emily Maddock

Joseph John Morgan to Edmund Morgan

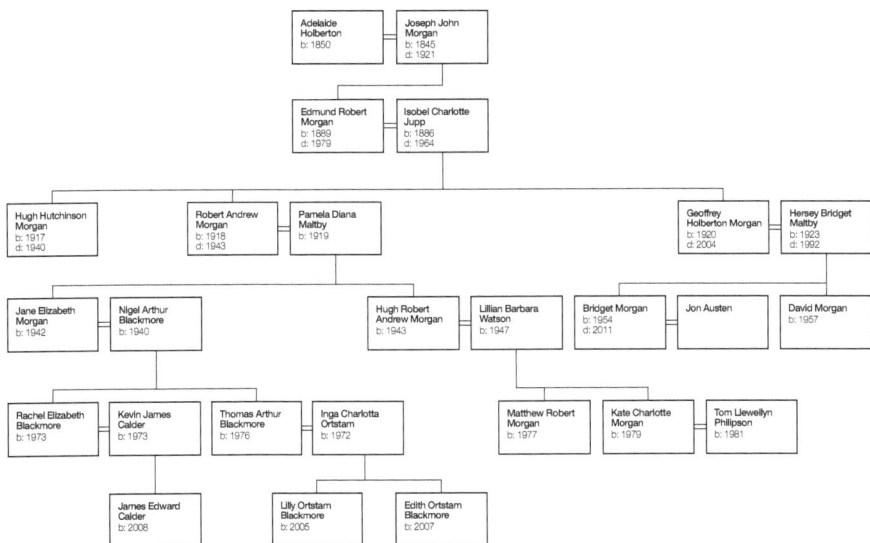

- Adelaide Holberton
  b: 1850
- Joseph John Morgan
  b: 1845
  d: 1921

- Edmund Robert Morgan
  b: 1889
  d: 1979
- Isobel Charlotte Jupp
  b: 1886
  d: 1964

- Hugh Hutchinson Morgan
  b: 1917
  d: 1940
- Robert Andrew Morgan
  b: 1918
  d: 1943
- Pamela Diana Maltby
  b: 1919
- Geoffrey Holberton Morgan
  b: 1920
  d: 2004
- Hersey Bridget Maltby
  b: 1923
  d: 1992

- Jane Elizabeth Morgan
  b: 1942
- Nigel Arthur Blackmore
  b: 1940
- Hugh Robert Andrew Morgan
  b: 1943
- Lillian Barbara Watson
  b: 1947
- Bridget Morgan
  b: 1954
  d: 2011
- Jon Austen
- David Morgan
  b: 1957

- Rachel Elizabeth Blackmore
  b: 1973
- Kevin James Calder
  b: 1973
- Thomas Arthur Blackmore
  b: 1976
- Inga Charlotta Ortstam
  b: 1972
- Matthew Robert Morgan
  b: 1977
- Kate Charlotte Morgan
  b: 1979
- Tom Llewellyn Phillipson
  b: 1981

- James Edward Calder
  b: 2008
- Lilly Ortstam Blackmore
  b: 2005
- Edith Ortstam Blackmore
  b: 2007

Joseph John Morgan to David Morgan

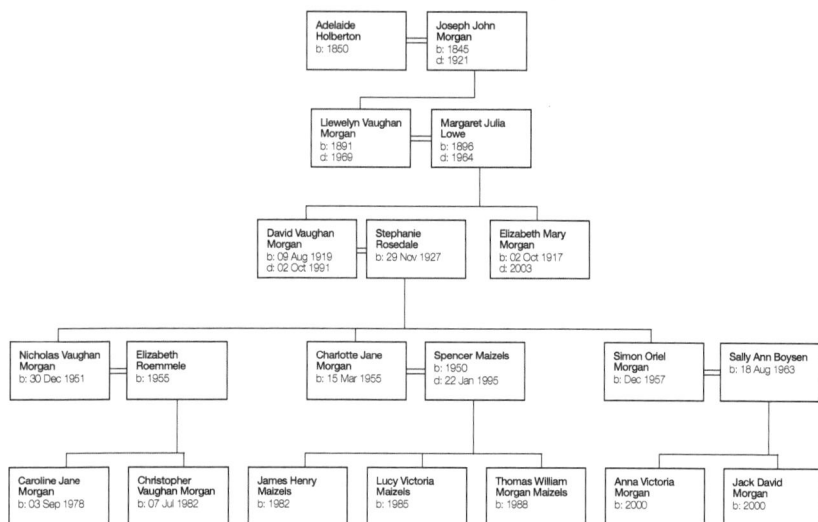

```
┌─────────────────┐ ┌─────────────────┐
│ Adelaide        │ │ Joseph John     │
│ Holberton       │ │ Morgan          │
│ b: 1850         │ │ b: 1845         │
│                 │ │ d: 1921         │
└─────────────────┘ └─────────────────┘
```

```
┌─────────────────┐ ┌─────────────────┐
│ Llewelyn Vaughan│ │ Margaret Julia  │
│ Morgan          │ │ Lowe            │
│ b: 1891         │ │ b: 1896         │
│ d: 1969         │ │ d: 1964         │
└─────────────────┘ └─────────────────┘
```

```
┌─────────────────┐ ┌─────────────────┐ ┌─────────────────┐
│ David Vaughan   │ │ Stephanie       │ │ Elizabeth Mary  │
│ Morgan          │ │ Rosedale        │ │ Morgan          │
│ b: 09 Aug 1919  │ │ b: 29 Nov 1927  │ │ b: 02 Oct 1917  │
│ d: 02 Oct 1991  │ │                 │ │ d: 2003         │
└─────────────────┘ └─────────────────┘ └─────────────────┘
```

```
┌──────────────┐ ┌──────────────┐  ┌──────────────┐ ┌──────────────┐   ┌──────────────┐ ┌──────────────┐
│ Nicholas     │ │ Elizabeth    │  │ Charlotte Jane│ │ Spencer Maizels│  │ Simon Oriel  │ │ Sally Ann    │
│ Vaughan      │ │ Roemmele     │  │ Morgan       │ │ b: 1950      │   │ Morgan       │ │ Boysen       │
│ Morgan       │ │ b: 1955      │  │ b: 15 Mar 1955│ │ d: 22 Jan 1995│  │ b: Dec 1957  │ │ b: 18 Aug 1963│
│ b: 30 Dec 1951│ │             │  │              │ │              │   │              │ │              │
└──────────────┘ └──────────────┘  └──────────────┘ └──────────────┘   └──────────────┘ └──────────────┘
```

```
┌──────────────┐ ┌──────────────┐  ┌──────────┐ ┌──────────┐ ┌──────────────┐   ┌──────────┐ ┌──────────┐
│ Caroline Jane│ │ Christopher  │  │ James    │ │ Lucy     │ │ Thomas       │   │ Anna     │ │ Jack     │
│ Morgan       │ │ Vaughan Morgan│ │ Henry    │ │ Victoria │ │ William      │   │ Victoria │ │ David    │
│ b: 03 Sep 1978│ │ b: 07 Jul 1982│ │ Maizels  │ │ Maizels  │ │ Morgan Maizels│  │ Morgan   │ │ Morgan   │
│              │ │              │  │ b: 1982  │ │ b: 1985  │ │ b: 1988      │   │ b: 2000  │ │ b: 2000  │
└──────────────┘ └──────────────┘  └──────────┘ └──────────┘ └──────────────┘   └──────────┘ └──────────┘
```

Joseph John Morgan to Prue Morgan

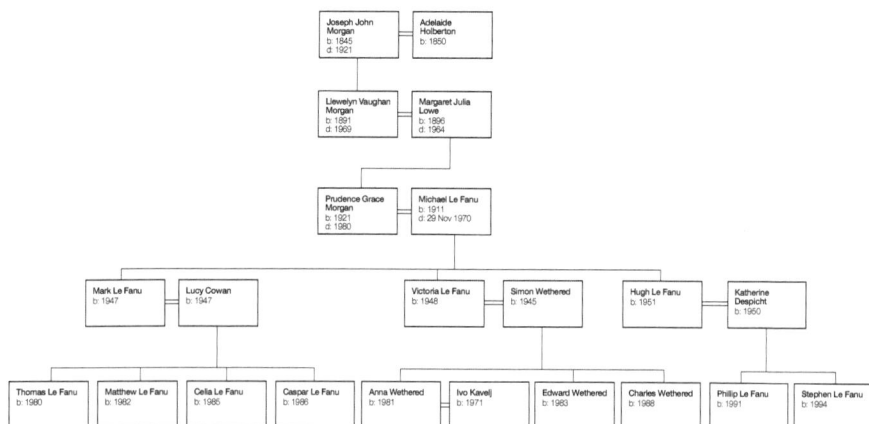

```
┌─────────────────┐ ┌─────────────────┐
│ Joseph John     │ │ Adelaide        │
│ Morgan          │ │ Holberton       │
│ b: 1845         │ │ b: 1850         │
│ d: 1921         │ │                 │
└─────────────────┘ └─────────────────┘
```

```
┌─────────────────┐ ┌─────────────────┐
│ Llewelyn Vaughan│ │ Margaret Julia  │
│ Morgan          │ │ Lowe            │
│ b: 1891         │ │ b: 1896         │
│ d: 1969         │ │ d: 1964         │
└─────────────────┘ └─────────────────┘
```

```
┌─────────────────┐ ┌─────────────────┐
│ Prudence Grace  │ │ Michael Le Fanu │
│ Morgan          │ │ b: 1911         │
│ b: 1921         │ │ d: 29 Nov 1970  │
│ d: 1980         │ │                 │
└─────────────────┘ └─────────────────┘
```

```
┌──────────┐ ┌──────────┐   ┌──────────┐ ┌──────────┐   ┌──────────┐ ┌──────────┐
│ Mark     │ │ Lucy     │   │ Victoria │ │ Simon    │   │ Hugh     │ │ Katherine│
│ Le Fanu  │ │ Cowan    │   │ Le Fanu  │ │ Wethered │   │ Le Fanu  │ │ Despicht │
│ b: 1947  │ │ b: 1947  │   │ b: 1948  │ │ b: 1945  │   │ b: 1951  │ │ b: 1950  │
└──────────┘ └──────────┘   └──────────┘ └──────────┘   └──────────┘ └──────────┘
```

```
┌────────┐ ┌────────┐ ┌────────┐ ┌────────┐  ┌────────┐ ┌────────┐ ┌────────┐ ┌────────┐  ┌────────┐ ┌────────┐
│ Thomas │ │ Matthew│ │ Celia  │ │ Caspar │  │ Anna   │ │ Ivo    │ │ Edward │ │ Charles│  │ Phillip│ │ Stephen│
│ Le Fanu│ │ Le Fanu│ │ Le Fanu│ │ Le Fanu│  │Wethered│ │ Kavelj │ │Wethered│ │Wethered│  │ Le Fanu│ │ Le Fanu│
│ b: 1980│ │ b: 1982│ │ b: 1985│ │ b: 1986│  │ b: 1981│ │ b: 1971│ │ b: 1983│ │ b: 1988│  │ b: 1991│ │ b: 1994│
└────────┘ └────────┘ └────────┘ └────────┘  └────────┘ └────────┘ └────────┘ └────────┘  └────────┘ └────────┘
```

A PASSING GUEST

1

A Career Start

"Who's the most junior nurse in this theatre?" roared the Ear, Nose and Throat surgeon, glaring round at his minions under his fearful eyebrows. He had just finished the first part of his morning's work which consisted of capturing pairs of children's tonsils with what looked, to my appalled eyes, like a small wire lasso. He dropped them into a blood-smeared bucket, where they bounced slightly, and tore off his gloves. These landed on the floor. The last of the small inert bodies was picked up and borne away on a trolley.

It was my first day of 'surgery'. I was nervously washing-up some of the gory instruments at a sink in the corner and trying to keep as low a profile as possible. The anaesthetist yawned languidly and leant back in his chair. He was evidently used to such explosions as the tension of the morning's work fell away. Everyone else proceeded confidently with their jobs, ignoring the outburst.

Mr Jason's eye fell on me. I was, quite clearly, the youngest and least important person in the theatre.

"Go and make some coffee, nurse," he shouted, striding off into the staff room and sinking into the only comfortable chair.

Where was the coffee? Where were the cups? Worst of all, where was the kettle?

I foraged wildly in various cupboards in a tiny room which passed for a kitchenette, haste making for less speed. Ah, a tray and some cups and coffee and here, at last, a kettle. I could hear impatient noises floating ominously from the staff room. The watched kettle took far too long to heat up and was about half boiled when I poured the hotish water over the coffee. Filled with trepidation, I deposited the tray on a table by Mr Jason and fled.

Minutes later there was a frightful bellow from the staff room.

"Tell that nurse she's not fit to get married, ever." The screech echoed down the corridor and, I was sure, filled the entire hospital.

Aged nineteen, I had survived a year as a student nurse at the well-regarded King's College Hospital, Denmark Hill. King's had been chosen by my parents for the simple reason that my godmother's husband, Dr Creed, whom I had hardly met and who I never came across in all my four years there, was the Senior Pharmacist. Since we seemed to have no knowledge of other training schools it was as good a choice as any and probably a good deal better than some.

King's had an outpost near Epsom, having taken over the disused mental hospital at Horton. A few junior months of our probationer-training took place there, in outdated wards with long, cold, echoing corridors connected by stone staircases. A visit alone on night duty, perhaps to fetch a trolley or to the mortuary to bring back a shroud, was a scary experience. Wrapped in a cloak against the chill and hurrying to avoid the ghosts which were, I knew, waiting menacingly round every dark and shadowy corner, it was a great relief to regain the dimmed lights of the ward and the company of colleagues.

The four medical students who had studies on the ward would break off from their books and come and lounge in the kitchen when I was cutting bread and buttering it for the morning.

"Can I sit in here for a bit?" Edward would ask. "It's so cold in my room – and what about a cup of tea?" No passes were made or, indeed, expected, for all the opportunities that night duty afforded. Edward felt that this needed an explanation. "We have a deal between us four," he said. "We find that we all rather fancy you, so the pact is called 'Hands off Steph'!"

"Oh," I said, completely taken aback and "Ow," as I cut my thumb with the bread knife. I began to feel like a paler version of the eponymous heroine of the 1911 book *Zuleika Dobson* by Max Beerbohm. She had so many of the young Oxford undergraduates in love with her, who, on being rejected, committed suicide *en masse* by jumping into the River Thames, that she ordered a special train – to Cambridge. She had not been in love and neither was I. But was there a tinge of disappointment in my inadequate response to this declaration of mass affection?

I expect Edward became a renowned physician or surgeon but he faded, unregretted, from my life and so did the other three. I went back to London for the remainder of my training, and the rest of my life began.

2

A Serendipitous Discovery

When I and my sisters and brother were attacking the task of sifting through the books and papers in his study after the death, in 1983, of our father, Rio Rosedale, we came across some jewellery which our mother had hidden among his books 'for safety' and had long since forgotten. In her later years many a carer was loudly suspected of stealing this cache.

"How lovely, darlings, to have it back. I always knew it would turn up one day," she remarked calmly, slipping on a ring or two.

We also found a manuscript of which we had previously known nothing. It was a long memoir of his life by our paternal great-grandfather, dictated to his daughter in his old age. We had never heard of this relation before, nor even of the great aunt, and now it was, frustratingly, too late to ask our father anything about either of them.

We learnt from this document that Rio's grandfather, Wilhelm Levi (or possibly Ludwig) Rosenthal was a Jew, born in 1820, a native of West Prussia. Wilhelm had been destined to become a Rabbi but, ignoring the strict Jewish rules of the time, he had eaten a meal with a Christian friend at University, and – a much worse sin – without his hat on.

Rumours of these serious misdemeanours raced back to his parents and their neighbours and a career as a Rabbi was denied him in his native country. He set off for America where he understood things were more liberal but fell among thieves when the ship paused in London. His expectation that Jews would be as honourable to a fellow Jew, as had been his life experience till then, was sadly mistaken. He could travel no further, being by this time destitute.

From an abandoned newspaper, read while he was having a frugal breakfast, he learnt that a tutor was needed in a College Don's family in Winchester to teach German. He applied with a penny stamp and, on being accepted for the post, travelled third class to Winchester. This cost him his remaining few shillings.

Here he was introduced to a colleague of his new employer, a fellow Jew who had converted to Christianity. Initially Wilhelm was horrified to learn of the conversion since such a move was anathema to the Jewish mind and race. However, he discovered that this new acquaintance had been influential in his gaining the post in Winchester; he had deduced from Wilhelm's name that he was a fellow Jew and wished to help such a one. A deep and important friendship followed which lasted for the rest of their lives.

This friend was instrumental in convincing Wilhelm of the truth, as he saw it, of Christianity. Much agonising soul-searching and mental anguish followed. The knowledge of the sorrow, distress and disgrace that conversion would bring to his Orthodox family in Prussia, made him so ill that he was forced, after a time, to leave Winchester. He was tormented by a story he had heard of another young man who had returned to his home after a similar conversion, only to be rejected by his parents.

This young man had knocked on the door of his home. It was opened by his father.

On seeing him, the father had said coldly, "I have no son," and had closed the door in his face.

However, Wilhelm was utterly convinced of the rightness of his decision to convert in spite of his family's pleas for him to reconsider. He worked with various Christian organisations in London, was eventually ordained and, much later, anglicised his name to William Lewis Rosedale. (Interestingly, I discovered that Adolphus, a brother of William's, who also travelled to England long after his elder sibling, had converted to Christianity as well and been baptised by him. According to the 1881 Census, the brothers had later moved to live next door to each other in Sydenham in south-east London, where William was the vicar of St Saviour's and Adolphus was a paper merchant.)

William became the vicar of Short Heath, near Wolverhampton, building a new church there and the vicarage. After a while he heard of a young lady, Caroline Gough, who was going about a neighbouring parish, delivering tea, sympathy and religious tracts to the families of 'navvies' who were then building canals in the Midlands. "She sounds just the wife for a clergyman," he said both to himself and a fellow cleric. This friend arranged for William to meet the family of the young woman and, far too precipitately, he announced his intentions. Unsurprisingly, this met with stony refusal from the rich and worthy parents, Mr and Mrs Ralph Dickinson Gough.

'We don't know anything about this foreign Jewish convert or his family,' they must have thought privately; 'Caroline is not going to marry him.'

Months later, her father and one of her brothers were in London, visiting their bank.

Knowing them well (how different from today!) and where they lived, the manager enquired whether they knew of a young clergyman in a nearby parish. "He is Jewish, and has converted to Christianity, much to the distress of his parents. We have done business with the family for many years and I am well acquainted with them. They are very distinguished and well-regarded in West Prussia."

This proved an auspicious and mind-changing meeting. Mr Gough visited William, invited him to dine and both parents agreed to the marriage. (After considerable research I discovered that Caroline's mother, Mrs Gough, our great-great-grandmother, had been born Miss Katharine Tunnicliffe. In 1939, one of her great-grandsons, Gerald Tunnicliffe, a second cousin of our father and also his personal solicitor, harboured us all in his country house near Marlborough on the outbreak of the Second World War.)

Both the two sons of this marriage were of the cloth and the younger, Honyel Gough Rosedale, was Rio's father. The daughter, Beatrice, married yet another clergyman, the Reverend Charles Upwood Manning, of Diss in Norfolk.

(Many years later, through a mutual friend, I traced and visited a second cousin, one Robert Manning, a solicitor, still living in Diss, who furnished me with the photograph of a painting of our mutual great-grandmother, Caroline Gough, wife of William Rosedale. The Mannings had, historically and for many decades (until Robert himself) been the vicars of that parish. He showed me the plaques to their memory on the walls of Diss church and with these and the respectful tone of the many greetings he received as we walked along, it became clear that he was in fact pretty close to being 'Mr Diss'.)

Why had we, as children, not asked about Rio's forebears? Why had our great-grandfather not even been mentioned and why did we never meet our great aunt and her children? Was our father silent because of the attitude of anti-Semitism that was wide-spread in the country when we were young? Perhaps he considered it safer, in a war that was killing so many Jews, that we knew nothing of our Jewish connections, however much diluted by three generations of English blood. After some research I discovered that in his extreme old age our great-grandfather had lived only a street away from his clerical son, our grandfather, Honyel. Both had been, in succession, vicars of the same church in Kensington Park Road. William died in 1904. Our father was then thirteen years old and must have known him well.

(Rio, though never a snob, seems to have been slightly more interested in, and closer to, his maternal, more landed-gentry and quintessentially English, Pelly relatives, than the equally respectable co-descendants of his Jewish grandfather.)

In 2007, my brother Barney and I spent several days in Poznan (now Posen) in the west of Poland to try to discover more about our forebears. Frustratingly, it was a 'needle-in-a-haystack' search, where the 'haystack' had been gone over thoroughly by marauding Nazi armies; Jewish 'needles' had been corralled into ghettos and concentration camps and most records of them destroyed. Such of these as remained and were available for research in the Record Office there, were written up by hand, the words almost indecipherable to non-German experts.

All was not lost. We walked about the pleasant old town and saw the places with which our great-grandfather in his youth, and his family, must have been familiar. It was a poignant journey – the memory of the war and anguished thoughts of what probably happened to our unknown relatives and thousands of others during it accompanied us. We visited the British cemetery. The line upon line of graves, filled mostly with young airmen, was a moving sight.

William's memoir is a fascinating window into another age and into the qualities and life and love of an ancestor of whom we had never before heard. It raises, however, many questions that can't now be answered since it is maddeningly silent on aspects of his life about which it would be enthralling to know more. (At one point he mentions, exceedingly briefly and without further comment, that he had been on a 'visit to my family'. I long to know what happened, how he was received, who went with him and a host of other details.)

I was spurred on by the discovery of the memoir to write this rather longer one.

3

Children of the Vicarage

The only child of Canon James Edwin Jagger and his wife Caroline Bertha née Edmonds, was our mother, Marjory Bertha – Peggy, as she was known, who was born in May, 1897. Her father's parish was in Bakewell, in Derbyshire, where they lived until she was about seven. He was then appointed to the living of St Mary's, Merton, on the edge of south-west London. A century before, Admiral Nelson and his Emma had attended this church when they lived together nearby in what was then considered sin.

Peggy's mother came from a family which can be traced back to the fifteenth century, many of the members of which lived in Devon. In the sixteenth century there was a Sir Thomas Edmonds, born in 1562, who was described by the Reverend John Price in his *Worthies of Devon*, as 'Knight and Controller of the Household of King James I'. He was first despatched by the King as ambassador to Brussels in 1603 and was recalled from a similar posting in Paris in 1616. His wife was a Lady-in-Waiting to the then Queen.

Their son, John Edmonds (1647–1731), owned and farmed the estate of Yetson near the village of Ashprington and his house still stands, overlooking Bow Creek, an estuary of the river Dart. He was the three times great-grandfather of Caroline, my maternal grandmother.

As with so many of my forebears, the family tree is dotted with clerical personages. Caroline's father, the Reverend Richard Pell Edmonds, born in 1831, was, with his three elder sisters, orphaned very early in life by the death of both his father Richard in 1832 and his mother Elizabeth in 1833. Elizabeth's mother, their grandmother, who had then taken charge of them all, died a year later. It was a pillar-to-post childhood for them all but Richard grew up to marry Fanny Arnold, born 1830, and to become the father of eleven children. Four of these moved to South Africa where countless numbers of their descendants live to this day, including the children of Lorna Playfair, one of his many grandchildren, who did much of the research for this information.

Another grand-daughter was my mother. An indulgent only-childhood and her own strength of mind together formed Peggy's robust, vigorous and energetic character. She trained as a social worker in London's East End and 'Hon Sec', (Miss Lockett, but never known by any other name) her mentor, team leader and friend, became godmother to my elder sister later. (It was in her cottage in Shamley Green in Surrey that we spent part of a wartime summer holiday – the only warm memory I have of that conflict.)

Geoffrey Baggalay, who was a barrister and a Regular in the Army, was also the brother of Peggy's great friend, Joyce. He had somehow survived the First World War, losing a leg and suffering many other brushes with death. Peggy and he had numerous interests in common. They fell deeply in love and became engaged in August 1920, delighting both their families. With the wedding arranged for the following May, he was sent to Ireland as a prosecutor on Courts Martial and was shot dead in Dublin by the Sinn Fein in November the same year, aged twenty-nine. There is no doubt that he was the true love of her life, his memory a perfection untainted by any possible later fallibility. This was a crushing blow and no-one, not even our father, could ever quite live up to Geoffrey's remembered flawlessness.

Peggy kept a diary of her love affair with him and of his death in Ireland, calling it *My Man* – a poignant story of great happiness followed by great sorrow. It was five years before she could contemplate another relationship, this time a rush into marriage with my father. She and her friend Joyce spoke sadly of Geoffrey, Joyce's only brother, and she became, eventually, another godmother to my elder sister.

Our father, William Oriel Pelly Rosedale – 'Rio' as he was known – was originally a Norfolk boy. He was born in 1891 in the village of Middleton, near King's Lynn and was the elder son of Canon Honyel Gough Rosedale and Ada née Pelly.

Ada's father, Percy Leonard, Rio's English grandfather, was the youngest child (of ten) of Sir John Henry Pelly, (1777– 1852) 1st Baronet, sometime Governor of the Bank of England (1841–1842) and Governor of the Hudson Bay Company from 1822 until his death thirty years later. Though he never ventured there, Northern Canada is dotted with his name. A Bay in Nunavut, an Island on the Arctic coast off the North-West territories, Lakes, Banks, a Crossing and a River in the Yukon, Pelly Mountain and Pelly Point on Victoria Island, are all named for the Governor.

He was the uncrowned king of half of Canada and received his baronetcy for organising another, this time successful, expedition (following Franklin's heroic failure to do so) to prove the existence of the North-West Passage in 1839.

Just as a sideline, he also fitted in being the Deputy Master of Trinity House, the UK's Pilotage and Lighthouse Authority. From St Martin's, in the Isles of Scilly, where many of my family have holidayed for twenty years or more, the towering Bishop Rock Lighthouse can be seen to the south-west, the building of which is said to have been John Henry's responsibility.

Rio Rosedale's other grandfather, William, the author of the memoir, had been the vicar of Middleton in Norfolk. Now his son, Rio's father Honyel, had succeeded to the living and here Rio was born and baptised. Later the family moved to Sydenham, London, where William became the vicar of St Saviour's. Rio and his brother Thorold were educated at the Merchant Taylors' School. Their younger sister Ursula, who (Rio wrote sadly, much later in life) was 'my closest friend', died tragically, aged about fifteen, at school in Germany.

Rio read Greats at Lincoln College, Oxford, and spent most of his spare time starring in the Oxford University Dramatic Society. On graduating in 1912 he joined the Nigerian Colonial Service. In 1906 Lady Lugard, wife of the High Commissioner in Nigeria, published her book, *A Tropical Dependency*. This was a history of that country and the setting up of the British Administration there at the beginning of the century, when most of Europe was scrambling to divide up Africa into their colonies.

In the book she recorded the high quality of the body of men under her husband's authority. She wrote:

The staff... was chiefly composed of that fine type of young Englishmen who... have it in their minds to serve their country to the best of their ability, in some adventurous capacity which will take them out of the common round of comfortable life... They were ready to go anywhere and to do anything... and represented, in the eyes of the High Commissioner, the very best stuff of which the English nation is made. He had in them the instruments that he wanted and he worked them without mercy, as hard as he worked himself.

Allowing for the slightly over-blown patriotism of the time, the young men who joined the Service when my father did, among them my future godfather, Charles Woodhouse, were of the same quality as those adventurers of a decade earlier. Nigeria was a well governed nation, in co-operation with the local chiefs, and was a fair and just place until Independence.

He remained in that country, which he came to love, for twenty-five years, rising to become Senior Resident, mostly working in the Muslim north – Kano, Kaduna and Jos were all names we heard bandied about as children. It is possible that he was in line to become Governor of Nigeria, but the Second World War wrecked his career as it did that of so many people.

Peggy set off by train from Liverpool Street to visit her parents, who happened at the time, September 1925, to be in Norfolk. There entered into the carriage a young man of attractive appearance whose blue eyes matched his tie and set off his tanned skin and fair hair. He sat down and, after enquiring whether she minded, lit a pipe.

"Are you going far?" he asked as an opening gambit. He had a pleasant voice.

"I'm going to King's Lynn," she said. "My father's doing a locum for a clergy family in a village near there."

'She's very pretty,' he thought. She was tall, dark-haired and brown-eyed with a lively, intelligent face and a good figure. (Of their future children, two had brown and two had blue eyes.)

"My father's a clergyman too, now retired," he remarked. "My parents are on holiday in Norfolk at present and I'm going to see them before my leave is over. I'm going back to Nigeria next month."

They discussed his work and hers and other subjects of

increasingly personal interest, the attraction fizzing between them. The train meandered pleasantly through Suffolk and, quite unnoticed by either of them, through the undulating small hills and flat plains of Norfolk.

At King's Lynn they alighted. "Which village are you bound for?" he asked, with scarcely concealed interest. He clearly meant to continue the acquaintance.

They discovered, of course, that both were bound for the same destination, the village of Middleton. It was a whirlwind courtship. They were married six weeks later, sailed for West Africa and the blue-eyed Diana was born after exactly nine months and one week.

4

My Beginning

It must have been the winter of 1930. It must have been a Sunday. I must have been nearly three years old. Winter, because it was dark so early – Sunday, because we always went to tea with my grandparents in their vicarage on that day and I was being bowled home in a pram. I peered out from the shelter of the hood and through the bare twigs and branches overhead, I saw the stars. This is my first memory.

My elder sister Diana was already in residence when I turned up, sixteen months later. Camilla followed me after nearly three years and, six years after that, with a last throw of the dice in an effort to produce a son, my parents struck lucky and Barney was born. Camilla had enjoyed the privileged position of the youngest child for so long that the advent of a rival – and a male one to boot – was viewed by her with something rather less than pleasure. She kept him firmly under her thumb and allowed him not the slightest sense of masculine superiority. He was, of course, the apple of every eye except hers, and her efforts may have contributed to the fact that he turned out even half decent.

My mother's father was the vicar of St Mary's Church, Merton for some thirty-five years, in the days when staying in the same living till death stepped in was quite normal.

He rode about his parish on a tricycle, acknowledging the greetings of his much loved and loving parishioners with a precarious wave.

My grandmother, who was quietly beautiful, wore greys and blacks with a tiny lace collar round her neck like a miniature fence with slivers of whale bone as 'fence posts'. She was 'delicate' and lay about on a sofa a good deal. Our mother, their only living child, (their first, a son, had died as a baby) took us to tea there every Sunday. The very minor turbulence produced by having three little girls to tea once a week was more than enough for her nerves to cope with.

We particularly liked a book our grandmother kept for us called *Tim, Toots and Teeny*, which featured black-cloaked-and-hatted villains carrying bags labelled 'Swag' or even 'Bomb'. We knew it by heart. And around Easter she would hide chocolate eggs in the shrubbery, in nice obvious places so that we could find them easily and pretend to be surprised. Christmas also had its traditions. A tray of raisins and sultanas, flooded with brandy and set alight on the hall table, tempted us to brave the flames as we darted in with our small fingers to snatch the fruit.

The vicarage itself remains a lovely memory, perfect in its then nearly rural setting and separated from the church by a wall with a stone arch. It was – is – a Queen Anne or Georgian house (though now divided into apartments) with a then generous garden where bees were kept, vegetables grown, a pony cropped the grass in a field, fêtes were held and trees climbed.

Any particularly significant house described in almost any book I read today is, in my imagination, adjusted exactly to the dimensions, the layout and the beauty of this building. It was here, when I was a gap-toothed six-year-old, that Diana and I were bridesmaids to a first cousin of our mother's, the daughter of Walter Edmonds, one of our grandmother's many brothers. Mildred had been brought up in sunny South Africa, so that the pea-soup fog that engulfed her wedding day, together with the particularly dreadful shade of green decorating her toothless bridesmaids, must have been a depressing beginning to her marital life. She married Graham Blandy, head of the family and firm which makes Madeira wine in Madeira, and they were to have a momentous influence on my later life.

My mother had settled near her parents because we were, in effect, a single-parent family. We only saw our father at eighteen-month intervals when he returned on leave from the Colonial Service in Nigeria after a three-week voyage on a ship of the Elder Dempster Line. At the time, knowing no better, we took this to be a perfectly normal arrangement. Looking back, it was our mother who had to take all decisions, major and minor, and who we sensed found it hard to hand over decision-making to a husband who was only present intermittently. For both of them it must have been a lonely life.

There was wild excitement in the nursery as the day of the arrival of this virtual stranger drew near, and, when very young, I remember entertaining a certain vagueness as to who this man was who was about to invade our wholly feminine world. Vast amounts of baggage, brought in from the taxi, lay about on the floor of the hall and, stumbling over and round it, we would be swept up into huge bear hugs.

There were presents all round, extracted with some difficulty, great delight and a good deal of noise, from the confusion of bags and trunks and cases. Strings of coloured beads, strange games involving beans, carved wooden stools and figures, African toys, lengths of cloth – all lay about in glorious chaos.

We were never taken to Nigeria. The white man's grave would certainly, it was thought, prove to be the white child's too. We were left to our mother's not always very tender mercies.

Her relationship with each of us varied. To her eldest she was undoubtedly domineering. Diana was quiet and, in a gentle way, obstinate, but was no good at confrontation. Our mother found her 'difficult', and even wrote to the Nursery World magazine asking for advice, comparing her unfavourably with the 'easiness' of her second child, me. Camilla was a different matter altogether. To her, rebellion and altercation were the breath of life and the noise of healthy rows rang round the house, each protagonist giving as good as she got. I learnt lessons from both sides and kept my head down. Later on, after we had moved to a larger house in Merton Hall Road (since demolished) the longed-for son was born. He was never spoilt but could do little wrong.

Tender or not, her mercies were a good deal more bearable than those of the Home For Children Whose Parents Were Abroad, where, for some appalling months, while she travelled to northern Nigeria (and probably succeeded in conceiving Barney), we three small girls were abandoned. It certainly felt like abandonment – we were only aged nine, eight and five.

The Home was to the west of Putney, in what is now the South Circular Road. We three slept in a row in a dormitory of about seven children. Its windows overlooked a neglected garden in which we occasionally played, and the back of another large house. Josephine, a little girl whose parents were in India, had lived in the Home for years. After dark she cried quietly and so did we.

Camilla wet her bed one night – a not unlikely occurrence in our troubled state. Someone must have rung a bell and a carer rushed in. "Out you get, you naughty little girl." Camilla was hauled out and stood shivering and weeping on the cold linoleum while the sheets were changed. I got out of bed and put my arms round her but was told sharply to "get back to bed".

"Don't you do that again," she was told before being bundled back unsympathetically, "or you'll have to sleep in a wet bed." Diana and I watched helplessly.

Our grandparents had ample space in the vicarage; there was a schoolroom there, a large garden and, in those days, a cook, a chauffeur called Leslie who doubled up as gardener, and a housemaid, our beloved Emily – 'Enimelly' as we called her. Possibly it was the 'nerves' and the 'delicacy' that prevented the obvious solution to our mother's absence.

I suppose, as children, that we took the arrangements and plans of adults in an unquestioning way, knowing instinctively that we had no power to make changes. It must have taken a long time for Peggy to forgive her mother for this but I have no recollection of her discussing it in our hearing.

We were rescued at last by a doctor friend of the family and taken back to our own home. At the risk of falling into the 'misery memoir' trap, this was 'frying-pan-into-fire' country. A housekeeper of Victorian appearance and views was installed and her mercies were a good deal less tender than either our mother's or those of the Home. I can recall with no difficulty, Camilla sitting in front of a lunch-plate of uneatable cold food, the clock on the mantelpiece standing at three, the winter evening beginning to draw in and finally, of her nose being held while she was forcibly fed. In the midst of an otherwise averagely normal and happy childhood, this was not a good time.

But – our mother came back, and Barney was born, we climbed trees in the garden and occasionally fell out of them; we played with the dog, a nervous Red Setter called Boy, who ate curtains and cushions if left alone; we loved the gardener and got in his way; we all had whooping cough and were sick in the flower beds and we climbed the fence and gave it to the

40

next-door children who were sick in *their* flower beds.

Peggy had simple but strict views on discipline. If we were all playing in the sandpit and one of us bit someone else's toes, as occasionally happened, the consequent scream would bring her round the corner of the house like a whirlwind. We were all slapped, regardless of who was the perpetrator and who the victim of the crime, and only then were questions asked. We learnt to keep our shrieks at a low volume.

Over Wimbledon Common we went frequently, our destination the Windmill, Peggy briskly pushing the youngest child in a pram, two others holding on valiantly to the sides, feet scarcely touching the ground for the speed of progress and Boy hardly able to keep up. Here we drew breath before charging back home across the golf course, golfers in their scarlet jackets suspending their game, amazed at the velocity of our passing.

As we reached what she took to be the age of discretion, our mother, daughter of the vicarage and an unquestioning Christian, considered it was time for us to learn the Catechism by heart. After our baths, wrapped in dressing gowns and clutching mugs of Ovaltine, we sat in front of the fire, energetically renouncing the devil and all his works, the pomp and vanity of this wicked world and all the sinful lusts of the flesh. It was not explained to us what these were. (Indeed, we could have gone to our much later weddings as ignorant as new-born infants for all the information we acquired from our mother. Fortunately, my later St Mary's school friend, Anne Kelly, had a useful older cousin Margaret, who enlightened us on the mysteries of sex. "Ugh, it sounds disgusting," I remarked, aghast, aged thirteen. "I swear I'm never going to do that." Happily, the usual hormones kicked in in due course, the idea grew less repellent and even rather desirable, and the normal delights were eventually discovered. The oath was forgotten.)

Every morning, we walked to Wimbledon High School for Girls – up the road, over the Southern Railway line on a footbridge and along Worple Road to the foot of Wimbledon Hill. Had it been any other girl's father who was asked to give a talk to the school about Nigeria, I should have enjoyed the occasion. To a nine-year-old, however, a parent is acutely embarrassing if he takes even a single step away from a perfectly decent and bloodless anonymity into the limelight. I probably heard not a word of his talk, squirming, as I was, with self-conscious discomfort. I was quite ready, of course, to shine in reflected glory when Rio was loudly applauded.

5

The War and Boarding School

Meanwhile, the Great Depression of the late Twenties and Thirties hung like fog over the Western world, the Spanish Civil War was fought and the impending Second World War loomed ominously in the middle distance. We knew very little of this.

Childish ignorance was eventually dispelled. We heard Peggy talking to Rio. "I can't face another war of any length alone with four children," she said understandably but career-wreckingly. In the summer of 1939, during one of his infrequent appearances in our midst, Rio agreed with her and never returned to Nigeria. It must have been a tremendous personal sacrifice. Destined, at the age of forty-eight, for high office in the Colonial Service, he was among the huge number of people whose careers were not only disrupted but destroyed. He had controlled and ruled vast areas of northern Nigeria, and the Army which he then joined, wasted all his great talent and experience. We saw little more of him over the next six years than we had before and our mother went on single-handedly bringing us all up.

At the end of August, with war certain, we drove down to Wiltshire. Here, Gerald Tunnicliffe, a childless cousin of my father, pursued, with his wife, a quiet and probably blameless life as a solicitor, in a country house in Chiseldon, between Swindon and Marlborough. (With our arrival, their peace must have been one of the first casualties of the coming war. This was declared, shortly after our arrival, to a tensely listening nation.)

I was despatched, at the age of eleven and without much warning, to join Diana at boarding school at St Mary's, Calne, in Wiltshire. I lay in bed weeping in the dark with home-sickness. Memories of my time in the Children's Home had not been forgotten.

We were the only girls whose mother had been so ill-advised as to supply us with the sort of old-fashioned underwear known as combinations and we longed to grow out of these questionably hygienic and embarrassing garments. Everyone else wore the more conventional, and therefore enviable, vests, knickers and Liberty bodices, which we coveted and did eventually achieve.

Every week we had to learn the Collect for that Sunday and be able to recite it if asked by our formidable headmistress, Miss Matthews – or Matt, as she was known covertly. The result is that these poetic words remain fresh in my mind to this day, but only for the weeks of term. Collects from Sundays which fell in the holidays are not nearly so familiar.

Miss Matthews was one of the great headmistresses of the twentieth century. She was appointed in 1915 to St Mary's when she was only thirty-two years old, to take over a little band of thirty-nine girls and four teachers in the middle of a war, in the middle of Wiltshire. She retired thirty years later soon after the end of yet another war, having transformed the school from its financially shaky start to one held in high regard in the educational world.

During my time at St Mary's there were 153 of us – the same number as the fishes in the New Testament account that were dredged up from the Lake of Galilee – a coincidence much enjoyed and exploited by Matt.

Matt was short and round-faced with fair hair done up in a loose bun. She was an innovator as to girls' education and successfully prepared candidates for the great Universities as well as encouraging outdoor activities and games. She could also be terrifying and, on being summoned to her room and seated on the fender-stool, one knew one was in for a hard time. She also had favourites of which I was not one and my sister, Diana, even less so.

The first Sunday afternoon of each term was enlivened by Matt gathering us all together and reading *The Highwayman*, by Alfred Noyce, our imaginations fired by 'the road as a ribbon of moonlight, over the purple moor', as 'the Highwayman came riding, riding, riding, up to the old inn door'. She read, too, *Flower in the Crannied Wall* by Tennyson. Ever since, seeing tiny plants clinging to inhospitable walls, I am back in that room called Gabriel, sitting on the floor, entranced. (Miss Ellinor Gabriel was one of the founders of the school in 1873.)

My own many attempts at poetry in my teens and into early adulthood are contained in a notebook I recently rediscovered. Most of them are excruciatingly, embarrassingly, bad. I knew nothing of life, death or 'ever-lasting' romantic love yet the 'poems' are full of these subjects and Nature. I will mortify myself with only one of these.

November Night
November sky, pale early star
And wind playing with smoke.
The tall gaunt trees are tossed and bare,
The grey clouds run amok.
So twilight cold it is outside,
So firelight warm within,
And now a weeping night has come
To drip against the pane.

The curtain's drawn; the dark's shut out;
But still it's crying there.
The haunting night is loud with wind
And the dark trees are bare.

I spent the entire war years at this school, joining the rest of the family for most of the holidays wherever evacueedom had taken them. It took them away from the dangers of suburban bombs to freezing cold cottages in Wales or various parts of the south of England, all, in my memory, equally arctic. Even our mother, whose lavish views on fresh air, open windows and cold baths we knew well, was forced to light a few fires and stop up some of the worst draughts to keep the blackout secure and us from freezing to death.

There was at least one warm summer, which we spent in Shamley Green, near Guildford, at the cottage belonging to 'Hon Sec', my mother's mentor from her early social work years. In my mind, I always place the hilarious cricket match described in *England, Their England* by AG McDonell, on the cricket pitch of Shamley Green, surrounded as it was, by tall elms and the murmuring of bees. Cold, however, seems to be my main recollection of those years.

One winter holiday we were staying in the chilly and echoing empty school where Peggy had received such education as girls did in her day. Somehow she had persuaded the then current headmistress to let us perch there during the holidays. I must have been about fourteen. At school we were reading *Moby Dick* by the American writer Herman Melville, with its multitude of sometimes symbolic characters including the terrifying Captain Ahab, and the first mate of the whaling vessel, the *Pequod*, called Starbuck. (Incidentally, the coffee chain 'Starbucks' is named after this man.) I woke in the night to hear my parents quarrelling, not for the first time.

"You're never here," cried my mother. "How can you

know what it's like trying to feed and look after four children, let alone keep them safe in a war?"

"You know perfectly well that I have no choice in the matter. How can you blame me for something that's not my fault? You're being unreasonable. You could have taken them all to your cousins in South Africa but chose not to."

"We wouldn't have seen you at all if I'd done that. You would have stayed on in Nigeria with the length of Africa between us."

"Well, you were the one who chose to come here to this awful place. Why don't you take them home and be more comfortable there?"

"Home? Comfortable?" Her voice rose. "Back to the bombs? How reasonable is that?"

"Don't shout – you'll wake the children." Their voices dropped to tense and worrying whispers which resonated in the bare spaces. I shivered in the darkness.

A few of my contemporaries at school came from broken homes and it was all too possible to conjure up the same frightening scenario, not helped by huddling in the dark and cold of a wartime winter night. I sometimes think that, had Peggy and Rio been of a later generation they might well, in late middle-age, have pursued separate paths. I mention this because, occasionally, whenever Moby Dick is mentioned I am back in that chilly empty school, listening, scared by hideous possibilities.

Cooking was never my mother's strong point. As a girl in the vicarage she had never had to do it, nor later in Nigeria on her visits there. One of the unrationed foods was fish – sprats figured in a big way on our menu. With very little familiarity with catering experience, she faced a formidable task in managing to feed us all in the dark days of the war, in circumstances of extreme difficulty.

"Could you join that queue for dog food," she'd say,

"and I'll go to the International Stores for the rations." Major, the dog, was quite resigned to what was probably horse meat, even though it was stained a lurid green to dissuade human beings from eating it. He was an independent dog of great character, given to long walks alone and therefore well-known in the area in which he probably found other kind sources of nourishment.

My father and I, when he was home for a brief leave, stood in the dark outside yet another rented cottage in the Surrey hills. Far away, searchlights roved about the sky to the north and a great glow lit the blackness. The bare trees were silhouetted against the lurid sky. Even at that distance, the grinding sound of the planes reached us from London – which was burning.

Occasionally, we must have returned to our home in Wimbledon, probably when the bombing was not quite so heavy. There was a precarious and probably groundless feeling of safety in the Anderson shelter in the garden. This would have been reduced to rubble by a direct hit, or even one down the road. The kitchen ceiling was reinforced with stout wooden columns round which we navigated with difficulty and in the tiny cellar there was a large tin of ginger biscuits which was apparently considered sufficient nourishment for a siege. We kept several hens in the garden at one time, in an effort to supplement the rations. Each occasional egg was reckoned to cost about ten shillings – a colossal sum in those days.

Back at school, in my fourth term – it must have been in January or February – I and the five others in my dormitory enjoyed a few days off school, having flu (or it might have been German measles). Anne had her well-worn cloth dog, McGregor, safely tucked up with her in bed. Julia enlivened us by accidentally tipping her almost frozen water jug all over her bed and we took it in turns to try and stay awake to keep a small and miserable fire alight through the night. Frost intricately patterned the insides of the windows.

Even in the safety of the country, air raid sirens wailed out from time to time and we were then instructed to file downstairs to the cellar, each carrying a suitcase already packed with spare clothes. On one occasion, after the roll-call, one person was found to be missing. "Where is Anne?" was the shout. Before a search party could be despatched, down the steps trotted Anne, quite unperturbed by the hue and cry, hair brushed, bright eyed, neat as a pin, carrying her suitcase in one hand and McGregor in the other. She had had to go back and rescue him since he couldn't, of course, be left to become a casualty of even an unlikely bomb. She and half a dozen others have remained my lifelong friends, though McGregor faded from our lives as we grew up, had other fish to fry and abandoned our furry friends in favour of the more masculine variety.

When we were all squashed blearily on benches round the damp walls of the cellar, Matt would read us something to keep us awake and reduce the boredom. To this day, the great, grey, green, greasy Limpopo River flows through that cellar, together with the lovely story and spelling of *The Young Visiters* (sic) written by Daisy Ashford, aged nine.

Whenever Winston Churchill was about to deliver one of his rousing speeches on the wireless, we were all corralled into the big room, Gabriel, to hear it. We sat on the floor, on the window sills, on cushions or squashed onto sofas and large chairs, silent while the sonorous voice inspired the nation to fresh efforts. Matt ensured that we kept well up to date with the progress of the war. Coloured pins on a map, moved back and forth with the contingencies of battle, marked the positions of our Forces in North Africa and other theatres of war. We followed them up Italy and were playing cricket on the top field, Lansdowne, when the planes roared over to support the D-Day landings.

We sometimes amused ourselves by speculating, in the dormitory after lights out, what our potential husbands were likely to be doing. We seemed to have no doubts that we were going to acquire such creatures sometime in the impossibly vague and distant future.

"I expect I'll marry an ambassador," mused the diplomat's daughter. "I think I'd like a farmer," dreamed a London solicitor's girl, tired of the fog and dirt of the capital. Resolutely reading under the bedclothes by the light of a torch, I usually plumped for a writer. As we giggled in the darkness, our prospective (and, indeed, eventual) spouses were almost certainly busy fighting a perilous war, in circumstances of far more danger than we could possibly imagine.

Several of my friends and I were roasting chestnuts over a Bunsen burner in the Lab. It was a particularly boring science lesson. We were taking advantage of the fact that Miss Winser-Aubrey, (pronounced Aubwey since she was unable to enunciate her Rs, and covertly known as Spawwow) was usually incapable of keeping order. Chestnut-cooking however, a culinary art not on the school curriculum, was evidently a bridge too far, even for her.

"This is too much," she said, bristling in a birdlike way with entirely righteous indignation. "I am sending you to Miss Matthews."

It was no laughing matter. We sat for a long time in Matt's waiting-room, silent with apprehension, while our nerves slowly shredded. This was easily the worst part of the punishment, as Matt no doubt intended. When the ordeal ended and she at last flowed in, like a ship in full sail, we were shivering wrecks.

"You will all spend this evening lamenting, like King Richard the Second in the Tower, the misuse of valuable and irreplaceable time," she announced. "You will write out a hundred times this appropriate quotation from Shakespeare –

'I wasted Time and now doth Time waste me'. But before that, you will go to Miss Winser-Aubrey and apologise for your bad behaviour."

We were more circumspect in our time-wasting after that.

My siblings and I learned four different musical instruments while our mother occasionally played the piano. Diana played the violin and continued to do so for life, Camilla the cello, Barney the flute, which left me with the viola. Our quartets, which were interrupted by squabbles about wrong notes, poor time-keeping, out-of-tune instruments and other more personal insults, were enormously enjoyable.

At school, the small rooms set aside for music practice overlooked the playing field and games of lacrosse were enlivened, or not, by the sometimes unmelodious noises emitted from the windows. Not a great deal of effort on my part was given to practising. I left school and scarcely touched the viola again. Singing was another matter – I was in the choir – and I have enjoyed that for most of my life.

Many a time I stayed in the holidays at the Dower House in Bartlow, near Cambridge, with my friend Catriona McCance (or Tree as she was always known.) She had an attractive elder brother, Colin, who was at school at Marlborough, just down the road from Calne.

Colin, a future doctor, was my first boyfriend, and later, when I was seventeen, he was the giver of my first serious, and delirious, kiss after a May Ball in Cambridge. Before this, even holding hands caused the pulse to race, so a first real kiss was heart-flutteringly exciting. I felt, at last, almost grown-up. (He, much later, became a consultant psychiatrist and lived in Scotland. His sister, Tree, has remained a friend to this day.)

Colin's friend, Ken, who had known Tree from childhood, was often there and she eventually married him.

The four of us sang madrigals endlessly and quartets from Gilbert and Sullivan. We taught ourselves the most intricate dance steps and swooped about the drawing room to records of dance music, concentrating on our feet, laughing and young and happy. In the evenings, nightingales sang in the wood opposite the house.

My friend Anne Kelly was the captain of lacrosse and I was the captain of netball. These exalted positions caused us to be chosen to take part in a live Children's Hour broadcast from Bristol on the subject of netball. It was extremely stilted since every word had been written out for us to read nervously into the microphone. Nevertheless, we were greeted back at school as celebrities. Matt, bursting with pride, declared, with rare praise, that I had sounded better than Alvar Liddell – a pin-up news reader of the time.

It was a very Church of England school. Quantities of time were spent in Chapel and every Sunday we crocodiled down to the Parish Church for matins, wearing our blue cloaks. We learned chunks of the Bible by heart, earning our 'Lilies' – a little blue 'shield' on a ribbon, on which these flowers were depicted – if we could recite them well enough. There was no discussion as to whether or not Confirmation was for you. Prepared by Matt, you just got confirmed, wearing your blue silk dress and an unbecoming white veil. It would have taken a far stronger soul than mine to resist this and at the time it never crossed my mind to do so.

Just as the war ended, I spent a few months at home waiting to be eighteen so that I could start my nursing training. (Someone had given me a nurse's uniform when I was seven and that had decided my career. The long forgotten donor could hardly have guessed the influence this gift would have on my future occupation.) During these months, to keep me occupied and, no doubt, to get me out from under her feet, my mother generously offered my services to a friend of hers who ran a small school. Every morning I caught a bus to Esher where what became an ordeal awaited me. The only benefit gained from this, for me or anyone else, was the certainty that the teaching of small children was not for me. Dropped into the deep end of a class of six-year-olds, who realised within two minutes that I had no idea how to swim in these waters, I was drowning. A good deal of noisy disorder ensued. I looked at my watch – ten minutes past nine. What felt like several hours passed and I glanced at the time again. It was twenty past nine. For some days this torture had to be endured until, fortunately, I caught the sort of cold that could be exaggerated into flu. "I am never going back there," I croaked, as firmly as a sore throat and blocked-up nose allowed. It was a great relief to be allowed to escape.

Still sniffling, but swiftly recovering on the promise that my fortnight's teaching career was at an end, my mother and I joined the celebratory street party that sprang up spontaneously when peace was declared. Lights were glowing from windows that had long been blacked out. Some people burnt their ration cards on the bonfire, which was ill-advised but understandable in the euphoria, as we needed them for many years to come. I stood sneezing in the warmth and brightness of the fire, feeling the almost tangible texture of delight and relief in the air.

In fact, in the period that followed, with the exhaustion of the population, the continued and indeed, expanded rationing which now included bread, and the huge debts incurred by the expenditure on the hostilities, Britain was a very grey place for a long time. Somehow with the resilience of youth, we accepted this and still managed to enjoy our lives.

6

Nursing Training

My first month's pay at the beginning of four years' training at King's College Hospital was three pounds, seventeen shillings and sixpence – about forty pounds a year. Admittedly we were fed and housed, uniformed and trained. But after six weeks' preliminary schooling we were let loose on the wards as very junior probationers and became completely indispensable, doing all the most menial jobs except sweeping the floor. This was done by ward maids who chucked used tea leaves under the beds to settle the dust before wielding large brooms. Sister Doris was my first Ward Sister and after more than sixty years I think of her almost weekly as I put away my clean towels, folded and stacked exactly so.

Her ward, which was run as a very tight ship, was a Men's Medical, usually holding about twenty-four old men, most with hacking, chesty coughs. Those with TB, in the days just before penicillin, streptomycin and other antibiotics, were pushed out in their beds, regardless of the weather, onto a roofed balcony overlooking the railway line. Strict order prevailed and routine was rigidly adhered to. No visitor was allowed in before the stroke of two pm and all were briskly ushered out as four o'clock struck.

Everyone was in awe of Sister Doris. "Have you nothing

better to do, Nurse, than talk to the patients? There's plenty of tidying to do in the sluice and then you could straighten all the lockers."

I have to say that I feel the training, in many ways, was considerably better than it is today. (No-one seems 'in awe' of the senior staff now.) Every four hours we went round with the 'Back Trolley'. Bed-bound patients had heels, elbows, shoulder blades and bottoms washed, rubbed and powdered and they were turned onto another side. A pressure sore, all too routine now, would then have amounted virtually to a capital offence; certainly it would have involved an interview with Matron, which amounted to much the same thing.

Of course there were more of us – as junior probationers we were, after all, pretty cheap labour – and there were far fewer forms to fill in and rather less technology to be learned. All the same, we were taught to nurse properly and really to care for the patients. This is sometimes not noticeable today. (There was in the curriculum a strange throw-back to the eighteenth century. Among the subjects with which we were expected to become familiar were 'cupping' and 'leeching'.)

In addition to the spell in the outlying Horton Hospital near Epsom, back in London we changed wards every few months. Many of the Sisters were pretty formidable. I was appointed to an orthopaedic ward, the Sister of which was notorious as a martinet and had a moustache to boot. I had had a grumbling appendix for some years which caused me no trouble at all. Now seemed the moment to make use of it. I called in at the sick bay, was in the operating theatre the next day, recovered, went on sick leave and returned gratefully to quite a different ward. Orthopaedics, as a result, was thereafter a closed book to me.

Night duty became our lot as we progressed through the training. During the third year, as a very young junior Staff Nurse, I would be in charge of a ward of some twenty patients. Sister Jane was the night Sister, the sight of whose approach on her rounds in the small hours caused the knees to tremble. Even if it was my first night on a ward, I had to know the name of every patient, every diagnosis, every prognosis and the treatment he or she was receiving. And still it was, "That locker isn't straight, nurse, and why are those flowers not taken out?" But when dramas occurred and the junior doctor on duty knew even less than I did, she would be there, calmly sorting things out, supportive and encouraging – a very great nurse.

Young doctors and medical students there were aplenty and we fell in and out of friendship and affection fairly frequently and perfectly innocently. I expect sex raised its head for some of my contemporaries from time to time but anything more than hugs and a bit of mild groping after a dance were beyond my, probably inhibited, youthfulness. There were dances and amateur dramatics and a certain amount of climbing back into the Nurses' Home long after curfew. There was a bit of kissing in the flower room, but never in the sluice. This disagreeable space was completely devoid of romance, being full of bedpans, sputum pots, urinals and dangling lengths of rubber tubing.

We were housed in the Nurses' Home. Long and expert practice over four years brought getting up in the morning to a fine art. The whole procedure could be accomplished in fifteen minutes flat – washing, dressing, brushing one's hair and running down to breakfast. We slogged through immensely long hours, often with lectures after work, and during these it was sometimes possible to catch up on some sleep.

Our clean uniforms were kept in a small room filled with lockers, which was usually locked but was opened up by the under-Matron, Sister Gladys, when we needed clean aprons. This room looked out on an inner courtyard some forty feet below. At right angles to the window was a wall with another casement about three feet away. I mention these details because there came an afternoon when the need for clean uniform in a hurry coincided with Sister Gladys forgetting to unlock the door. Several of us gathered at the second window, desperate to get at our clothes in time to be on duty.

I calculated the distance between the two window sills and tried not to look at the considerable drop to the flagstone courtyard.

"You can't do it. Don't, you'll fall and be killed," quavered my horrified friend, Joanna.

I climbed out, took a mighty step over the void to the other, open, window and grasped it. (The memory of this idiocy brings me out in a cold sweat to this day.) Hardly had I scrambled in, pulse racing and relieved still to be alive, when I heard the door being unlocked and the light was turned on. A flurried Sister Gladys entered, apologising to a queue behind her for being late, and I just had time to dive behind a row of lockers to avoid being seen. She was followed in by a surge of girls wanting their uniforms, amongst whom I merged with an air of completely false innocence. Joanna, looking as white as our clean aprons, was one of them.

"Don't you ever do anything like that again," she whispered fiercely into my ear as I mingled with the throng. "I don't know about your nerves," she added, "but mine certainly couldn't stand a repeat performance."

We burnt our candles at both ends and occasionally in the middle as well. It was possible to go clanging up in a tram to the West End and queue for a hard perch high in the 'gods' of theatres, costing all of half a crown (about twelve and a half pence) to see and hear more plays and musicals than I have ever managed since. *Oklahoma* was a tremendous hit in the post-war world. Its tunes and lyrics and the wonderful dancing brought unaccustomed colour and fun into London lives.

I had been to a film with Rebecca, a fellow nurse,

and afterwards we decided to walk back to the hospital, undeterred by the fact that it was now raining. This plan was defeated by the chance meeting with Dr John and his friend Dr Monty, both Junior Housemen. They were off-duty and had no difficulty persuading us to join them in Lyons Corner House in Piccadilly.

"Matron accused me of being drunk the other day," said Monty, stirring his coffee.

"And was this accusation justified?" I enquired politely, stirring mine.

"Oh yes," said Monty casually, "but I didn't realise it *was* Matron until too late. I can dimly recollect that she asked me if I was responsible for the unseemly noise – which, of course, I denied, but as there was no-one else in sight she didn't believe me." This was not surprising, Matron being a pretty sharp operator.

The two young men had watched a rugby match that afternoon, which the hospital had won. It had evidently been an unusual occasion. Fifteen years had passed since such an event had occurred.

"If we can keep up this standard," said John, hope triumphing over experience, "we might have a sporting chance of winning the first match in the first round of the Hospital Cup."

"How many rounds are there?" asked Rebecca.

"About five," said John dejectedly. We were not impressed or hopeful. He produced from a pocket some melting and rather fluffy chocolate which cheered us all up immensely.

In the last year of my training, I was a senior Staff Nurse. The Medical Superintendent arrived to look round the ward when I happened to be in charge and addressed me, to my gratification, as 'Sister'. The effect was somewhat spoiled by the smothered snorts of laughter from my so-called friends, John and Monty.

They qualified eventually and we parted from each other in a flurry of 'let's keep in touch', which we were too full of our future lives to fulfil.

'Doing the flowers' fell to my lot from time to time. I brought the vases into the ward and distributed them, as far as possible, to the rightful owners. This was not easy since a vase would either be disowned by the entire ward or else claimed by four people.

"Where are my chrysanthemums with the beech leaves?" enquired Mrs Arding.

"I'm afraid the flowers are dead and I combined the leaves with another vase," I explained.

"They were all right yesterday," she objected sniffily. Recklessly I offered to retrieve them from the dustbin, but she said, "Oh no, I'm sure you're right, nurse," in a voice and with a look that belied her words.

In the men's ward next door, 'doing the flowers' was a completely different experience. There, they consisted of three vases of nearly dead chrysanthemums and one with five carnations. I rescued these and since no-one so much as looked up from their newspapers, let alone complained, I gave them to an old man whose birthday it was.

7

Romantic Complications

My very first venture abroad was not long after the end of the war. As soon as it was possible to visit the Continent I travelled with my parents by train to Switzerland when I was twenty. It wouldn't have occurred to them to go there for the skiing so this was in the summer. People leaving Britain on holiday were allowed to take only twenty-five pounds each out of the country. (This did go considerably further than it would today. Such a sum nowadays would hardly get you as far as Dover.)

In our carriage there was a large woman with scarlet lipstick and bulky furs, who completely underestimated the calibre of my father, Rio. She kindly translated, for our benefit, the French conversation of a fellow traveller who was waxing lyrical on the beauties of the weather and the countryside. Rio bided his time, smiling quietly as she stumbled on.

"*Comprenez vous, Monsieur, Madame, Mademoiselle? Il dit qu'il fait beau, n'est ce pas?* That is ze weather is fine, you think?"

We politely did understand and we did so think, as we watched the sunny fields whiz by and ate our sandwiches.

Rio finished his last biscuit. Unhurriedly, he took part in the chat. Speaking perfect French, he and the Frenchman conducted a spirited discussion on the merits of French wine over that of Germany, at which the kindly erstwhile translator opened her mouth but was silent. The gentlemen parted, as we arrived in Lucerne, with many expressions of goodwill and with courteous thanks to the lady.

On arrival at our hotel my mother's luggage was found to be missing. It was, according to her, 'a disaster'. It would never be seen again. You couldn't trust 'foreigners'. What was she to do without it? The holiday was already ruined. She wished she had never come.

The Manager was sent for. "Madame," he soothed quietly, "no luggage is ever lost in Switzerland. It is temporarily mislaid, for which I apologise deeply. It will be with you within the hour." He retired backwards from her sceptical presence like the Cheshire Cat, leaving a 'smile' hovering in the air. Half an hour later a flunky appeared with the precious suitcase, followed by the Cat who was trying in vain to conceal a smug 'I told you so' look. He collected his floating smile and withdrew.

Mollified, Peggy was prepared to enjoy herself. We walked over the famous covered wooden Kapell Bridge and excursioned about the vast Lake Lucerne on a steamer, admiring the ring of mountains. We ate huge amounts of unrationed chocolate and we climbed to the top of Mount Pilatus and took the railway down again. It was on this expedition that we met another English family with a son of about my age called Tim Ormerod. He played the clarinet in the Scottish National Orchestra.

He eventually turned up back in London and because, charming though he was, I was not in the least emotionally interested in him, he had to be disposed of as gently as possible.

Other romantic connections complicated my life during this time. Two aborted engagements littered the scene, one to Sholto Scott-Watson, a London solicitor. How he entered our lives is lost in the mists of time. Initially, he was thought by the family to be interested in Diana, my elder sister, but having been kindly brushed off by her, he turned his attention to me. Aged about twenty, I was fancy-free and I enjoyed his company. We used to meet, when I was off-duty, in the Cardoma Café in the Strand, drink Lapsang Souchong tea and plan a possible future. It was not that he was a haemophiliac that brought this affair to an end but my realising that I was too young and far from ready for a lifelong commitment and not, actually, in love with him. There was a painful parting, a returning of the ring and a lightening of the heart – on my part at least.

I can now hardly remember Michael Duxbury. We must have been introduced and have met from time to time and I said "Yes" to his proposal after a party and a minor session in the parked car on the way home. I don't seem to have regarded this too seriously and neither of us took any steps to proceed with the affair. But when my official engagement to someone else emerged a few months later in the newspapers without any warning, he appeared deeply dismayed and I felt extremely guilty. Even now I occasionally reflect remorsefully on this discreditable episode.

8

My Father

At the end of the war, Rio's wide administrative experience –
he had ruled, as the Senior Resident, vast areas of Nigeria for
many years – was at last recognised and he was appointed to
the Control Commission in Germany. This organisation helped
to get that country back on its feet. He then left the Army and
joined the Civil Service in London and it was during my years
at King's that I began to get to know my father. If I had time
off during the day, we would often have lunch together. In
summer we sat on the grass by the river, eating sandwiches in
the shade of the trees by the Houses of Parliament.

"I have bought a set of First Editions of Jane Austen,"
he said proudly one day. He haunted antiquarian bookshops
and talked of books and his latest purchase of the Classics,
or the most recent green thriller Penguin, or of crosswords,
for which he had a passion – the harder the better. He was a
gentle, quiet man of great intellectual ability. When he retired
from London he taught Greek, Latin and French at a boys'
prep school in Wimbledon, the headmaster of which was a
close friend, and when at eighty, he finally gave even that up,
he was still fit enough to be presented with a bicycle. I chose
my parents well – I have very good genes.

Rio was much influenced by the two hundred years of

loyal service of his Pelly forebears. They had served the State and Empire in various capacities at home, in India, in both the Navy and the Army and in other spheres of useful life. In an eight-page *Account of Myself*, written sometime in the Sixties or Seventies, this tradition inspired him to:

> ... *treat my work in the administration of Nigeria as a Social Service and the people of that wonderful country as my children. This attitude is now frowned upon as paternalistic, but surely a father should do his best for his children and we were training them to stand on their own feet and... eventually to be able to govern themselves... But sixty years was not long enough.*

He spoke of his much loved Nigeria with protective affection and considered that the proposal for its independence after the war was premature. I contended with youthful arrogance that most Nigerians would probably prefer to make their own mistakes than be governed as a colony, however benevolent the colonists.

"They are not ready for it yet," he reiterated, possibly foreseeing what would later become of that country.

With only a childless uncle and no aunts on either side and therefore without first cousins, we had been brought up through the war with all its difficulties, bravely and, apart from school, almost exclusively by our mother. There were no loving relations to whom to escape and our father had been mostly absent in our childhood and teenage years. After the war, in my early adulthood, my father and I became better and more lovingly, and on my side at least, more admiringly, acquainted. In return, he was immensely proud and encouraging of us all.

He and I went Youth-Hostelling in the Lake District. There was no age limit to prevent anyone not exactly youthful from staying in these havens for walkers and Rio was probably in his late fifties. The only restriction then was that one had to arrive on foot – wheeled transport was frowned on. The hostels then varied wildly in their standards of discomfort. At the head of dramatic Wast Water we stayed in the Black Sail hut. This had probably been the home of some hardy eighteenth century shepherd, the ablution arrangements of whom we had no choice but to emulate. We washed in an icy trough outside the back door.

"If you do the washing-up," I instructed my father, "I'll peel the potatoes." (I could do this indoors in the comparative warmth while the washer of dishes had no alternative but to brave the outside chill. This was part of the YHA deal in those days.)

Lugging backpacks, we had walked from Ambleside, crossing Wrynose and Hardknott Passes and had spent a night in Boot, replenishing strength at its pub with welcome food and drink.

We strode on beside deep Wast Water, dark, mysterious and remote. (There was no question of arriving on wheels – the road ran out long before we got to the head of the lake.) On the opposite side of the water the enormously tall, bleak scree plunged vertically into what seemed a profound and bottomless narrow sea. Even the comfortless hostel was reached with pleasure.

We scrambled up Great Gable, descended to Borrowdale and caught a surreptitious and frowned on bus going towards Keswick, into which we sank as if relaxing in the most comfortable of armchairs. At the foot of the lane leading up to Watendlath we reluctantly took to our legs again. The reward was to reach a remote and lovely small 'hanging' valley with a picturesque tarn from whose calm waters the Falls of Lodore make their roaring way down to join Derwentwater.

Among our achievements were the ascent of Helvellyn and the scary traverse of Striding Edge – that razor-thin path in the sky which teeters between vertical drops to valleys far below. A strong wind, one felt, would send one careering into the next world. All this time we talked and talked. It was a very special time and an opportunity for bonding at last with my much loved father.

Rio was seldom, if ever, bored. He became a magistrate in Wimbledon and would return from the sessions with tales of the mostly minor misdoings of burglars, speeders and alcoholics. His view of the police was that they were almost always right. It was unthinkable for him to contemplate the possibility that lying or corruption could creep into their organisation or evidence.

He could escape into his study with his first editions, his green Penguins, his crosswords, all of Jane Austen's works and almost anything about her that was ever written. He entertained the Wimbledon Literary and Scientific Society on several occasions with elegant talks on her life and writings – his favourite subject. He was a Freemason and would go off to secret meetings carrying a suitcase with the necessary regalia, to much hilarity from his descendants. It was in his blood. His father had been the head of a Lodge.

For someone of ninety-one, his funeral in 1983 was extraordinarily well attended – he had been known and loved by a wide circle of friends and admirers.

9

My Mother

My one day off a week was sometimes extended by going off-duty at six the evening before and having the morning after free until eleven, thus enjoying two nights at home. I listened with envy to friends whose mothers brought them breakfast in bed on these precious days off. Needless to say, no such practices occurred in our house, though the occasional hot water bottle was left in my bed if I was expected home late.

"We can't sit here all day," our mother would say, gathering up the plates and teacups, as we tried to prolong chatting over breakfast, "there's everything to do" – a quotable family phrase to this day.

Peggy had never learned to cook since there was no need either in the vicarage or in Nigeria. In her old age, when we visited, she never economised on excellent ingredients but when the leg of lamb went into the fiercely hot oven it was accompanied by the plates, the surfaces of which were crackled from years of intense roasting. The cabbage was put on to boil at the same time thus reducing the Vitamin C content to nil and filling the kitchen with a familiar scent.

She continued her social work during our childhood and would take us along when she visited people with TB. The result in my case was that when tested at King's before beginning my nursing career, I had a very large reaction – clearly I had built up a huge immunity to the disease.

The Wimbledon Guild of Social Welfare was a lifelong interest to her. Well into her eighties she would drive people to Darby and Joan teas. "Dear old things," she would say on her return, "they do so enjoy these outings." We managed not to point out that quite a few of them were several years – sometimes decades – younger than she was. Age was an idea to be put at the back of the mind and ignored. (I follow her example in this regard.) Bright colours flashed through all her clothes and it was only when disabilities eventually made themselves felt that she remarked sadly, "Don't ever get old. There's nothing to be said for it." A series of resented helpers lived in, many loudly accused of stealing her jewellery. "When is that woman leaving?" resounded loudly through the house.

All the daughters visited as often as work and families allowed. The favourite and only son would also drop in on his way to some meeting in London.

"Barney was here last week," she would say, glowing with pleasure at the memory of his visit. "He's always so amusing and it was lovely to see him."

"No, I don't think so," she would reply vaguely, to enquiries by kindly neighbours as to whether the 'girls' had been to see her lately. I felt a touch of sympathy with the elder brother of the Prodigal Son.

A fall dealt her a severe blow. She broke a hip. Hospital was followed by a few months in a Nursing Home convenient for me to visit, in nearby Midhurst. By this time her life had no quality and she was almost blind with glaucoma. I saw her almost daily on my way home from work, anguished at her misery.

A phone call from the Irish Matron of the Home informed me that my mother had pneumonia. "But don't you worry, Mrs Morgan, I've got her on antibiotics and she'll be right as rain."

Back she struggled from near death. When a few weeks later a fresh bout of pneumonia threatened, I phoned her doctor.

"If you decide not to give her any antibiotics," I said, "none of us is going to sue you."

The Matron was horrified. Our mother died peacefully in December, 1988 aged ninety-one.

10

Finals and David

Finals for me at last. The Christmas number of the *Hospital Gazette* came out and to my astonishment and that of my relations and friends, it transpired that I had won a top award. This was the Monk Memorial prize – for, the certificate flatteringly says, 'general proficiency, excellent conduct, loyalty and devotion to professional duties' and, obviously, for not having been caught climbing in late at night and other misdemeanours. I was spewed out into the world as a fully qualified State Registered Nurse in January 1950.

I had booked a six month course in Part One Midwifery at the Radcliffe Infirmary in Oxford for the following May to top up the State Registration. The prospect of the five months gap before this began was heady.

My parents had bought a small house in Broadstairs to which we ventured for the occasional holiday. The family car was piled to the roof with luggage; my mother sat in the front with the petrol can under her legs and the cat basket on her lap. This contained Poppet, the cat, who complained loudly and unceasingly for the whole journey. Barney, aged about twelve, sat in the back with a mattress, five blankets, three suitcases, two boxes of food and several tennis racquets. His hamsters cowered in their box on his knees and Major, the dog, lay on his feet.

"Major is going to be sick," announced Barney, with about half the journey done.

I stopped the car and gazed at the dog but beyond an air of deepest dejection and despair, he appeared well. We drove on.

"Stop," cried Barney, a few minutes later, "the dog has *been* sick."

We coped with this as best we could in the crowded circumstances while Barney conveniently disappeared into a field on the pretext of taking Major for a convalescent walk.

'Twas ever thus – and we learnt to take precautions against dog-nausea on future occasions.

Freed from the rigours of the hospital, I ventured for the first time onto the ski-slopes – via my first flight – with Anne Kelly, my old school friend, who had followed me as a student nurse to King's. We flew to Arosa in Switzerland where I sprained an ankle, fell briefly in love with Rudolph, the ski instructor, and decided that skiing would play as large a part in my life as time and cash allowed.

Mildred Blandy, of the foggy wedding and the bottle green bridesmaids, now invited me to stay with her and Graham in Madeira.

'There aren't many young things out here,' she wrote, 'so I suggest you come when the Navy will be making a visit to the island. It should be more fun for you.'

Our grandmother, who died in 1943, left each of her four grandchildren a thousand pounds – a large sum then, the equivalent now of about twenty-nine thousand pounds. Little could she have foreseen to what extent this would affect my life. I used some of this to pay for the passage on the Warwick Castle to Madeira and spent most of the voyage lying in my cabin, pea green, having lost all faith in seasickness pills, as we heaved our way across the Bay of Biscay. I emerged, delicately pale, just before the ship arrived in Funchal.

The first sight of Madeira in the long-shadowed early morning light, with Funchal rising from the harbour up steep slopes scattered with white houses, was spell-binding. Boats hovered round the ship like floating seagulls, filled with small shivering boys who dived for pennies. The deck was strewn, by crowds of importunate Portuguese, with colourful and elaborate embroidery and straw hats. Graham swept up in his launch, passed the time of day with the Captain and whisked me off in an enormous car, up the hill.

The Blandys lived in a large house, Quinta do Palheiro, said to be the most beautiful on the island (it is now a hotel) with a splendid view overlooking the town and the harbour. A winding road led up to it. The garden was, and is, famous. Camellias and magnolias of all colours flourished among the tall trees, mimosa hung, brightly yellow against the bluest of skies, huge bunches of violets were picked daily for the house, lilies and orchids were everywhere and freesias, wild in the grass, were as lush and plentiful as English buttercups and smelled wonderful.

The contrast with the still grey post-war world at home was startling. My clothes, straight from rationed Britain, were, I knew, woefully inadequate, but in spite of this, I dropped blissfully into an unaccustomed life of luxury – wonderful food that I had forgotten or never known, beach picnics, swimming, tennis in the sunshine, 'green days in forests and blue days at sea'.

The Navy was scheduled to visit the island for four days. No effort was being spared for their entertainment. On the first day, the Cruiser HMS *Superb* and the Destroyer HMS *Crossbow* appeared in the early morning, wallowing far out in heavy seas. A polite salute of gun-fire was exchanged and away they sailed to shelter in nearby but less dangerous waters. No landings were possible.

"What a disappointment for everyone!" Mildred wailed.

"You've come all this way, and now they may not arrive at all and all the preparations will be wasted."

A heavy cloud of gloom descended on Funchal. A fork-lunch had been prepared at the Palace to which Graham and Mildred, with me attached, had been invited. Clearly the food had to be eaten but it was a half-hearted affair. Only faint hopes existed that lunch the next day with the Blandys would survive.

The next morning (19th February 1950) the sun had reappeared, the wind had dropped, the sea was unruffled. Mildred breathed a sigh of relief as HMS *Superb* steamed slowly into the harbour. The Admiral and his staff of four other officers made the rounds of official visits to the local dignitaries and then came up the hill to have lunch at Palheiro. They were all swooningly elegant in their white tropical uniform and amongst them was the tall figure of the handsome young Flag Lieutenant, decorated charmingly with the gold shoulder-tassels that depicted his role.

I was seated between the Admiral and 'Flags'. Conversation on both sides was easy but between David and me there was the beginning of attraction – a kind of chemistry. We were both fairly easy on the eye, as they say, and I could see Graham's raised eyebrow and quizzical smile directed at me from his end of the table as he took in the situation.

The Admiral invited me, personally and gratifyingly, to accompany Mildred and Graham on board the *Superb* for lunch the next day.

"This can be arranged," the Admiral's Secretary told me, solemnly and straight-faced as we all walked in the garden after lunch, "but only at great personal inconvenience."

I offered hastily not to come.

"Oh no, Admiral's Orders," he replied.

The next day I fell in love.

It was a whirl of social activity. We arrived on board

for the lunch, the Admiral greeting me with a query as to whether I was going to behave. "Yes, of course, sir," I replied with great dignity. "You don't look as if you are," remarked the Captain, quite unnecessarily.

When we left I enquired of the Admiral if I had behaved well and he said, "Beautifully," nick-naming me privately to Mildred as the 'Snotties' Delight', which annoyed me very much.

In the evening, after dinner at Reid's hotel, we joined the Admiral's party at the Club Funchalense, where David and I danced every dance and had to sit out on the balcony, romantically, to cool off.

Mildred and I played tennis with some friends the next day. I played atrociously. "Your mind is on 'other matters'," Mildred remarked with some truth. The reason for this was that I had had a message from David asking me to dinner à deux at the Savoy for that evening. I wore, with some pride, a dress I had made from lace taken from a garment which had belonged, decades previously, to my grandmother's youth. I recall it now with some embarrassment but at the time I felt really pretty.

We danced and laughed and fell more and more in love and enjoyed the sort of evening that one never forgets.

"I cannot, of course, possibly afford to get married," he remarked as we danced to such music as *Begin the Beguine* and, appropriately, *Some Enchanted Evening*. I took this to be rather a 'good sign'. The idea of marriage had clearly entered his consciousness. I therefore ignored his statement and by the time HMS *Superb* sailed away later that night, I felt pretty certain where both our futures lay. His cable from the ship and my first love-letter (I have it still) and, eventually, meetings back in England, confirmed that he knew as well.

It's difficult to understand why, logically, one person, potentially available and however pleasant, leaves one emotionally uninvolved and another grabs one's heart and makes off with it. David was thirty, I was twenty-two – perhaps we were both at exactly the right stage of our lives to think about a possible future together – though I, at least, was being swept along by excitement, emotion and love and was in no state to make decisions, vital or not. Those would come later.

It was intoxicating to be so happy.

I was subjected to much teasing by an amused Graham.

"David Morgan," he mused the next day, after the ships had steamed away, "let's see if his father's in *Who's Who*." He reached for a well-worn tome and thumbed through the Ms. "Ah, an entirely suitable retired and knighted Vice-Admiral with a wife, two daughters and one son, living in Hampshire. My considered opinion," he joked, "is that we can approve of this possible liaison!"

"And," he went on, "here's one of the Admiral's brothers – Edmund, Bishop of Southampton."

"Bishop of Southampton?" I exclaimed, "I've stayed in his house! Doesn't he live in the Close in Winchester?

Graham studied the book. "He does indeed," he said, "how did that come about?"

"One of my fellow students at King's is his wife's goddaughter. Stella was asked to stay there for a weekend and told to bring a friend. She took me. So it turns out, astonishingly, that I met his uncle a couple of years before I met David." In addition I had also met the Bishop's widowed daughter-in-law, Pamela, (whose husband, Robert, had died at sea in the Dodecanese in 1943) with her two children; Jane aged about six and Hugh about five. Uncle Ed's eldest son, also Hugh, had been killed as well, leaving only the youngest, Geoffrey, (married to Pamela's sister, Hersey) who was to play a loving part in my life much, much later.

"Well, well," said Graham, "that seems a good enough omen for the future."

11

Three Weddings

The midwifery course at the Radcliffe in Oxford began in May, 1950. It normally consisted of two parts. The first six months of training were undertaken in the hospital. The thrill of seeing a baby born for the first time – a whole new person coming into the world, albeit yelling and streaked with blood – was only exceeded by the relief and intense pleasure of the new mother. The second half of the course was always carried out in the community but circumstances and my future changed swiftly.

David spent much of the summer away on the Summer Cruise to Scandinavia, but when not at sea he took to visiting his long-unvisited Aunt Mary, who lived, conveniently, in north Oxford. She was the childless widow of a Professor of Hertford College whose much admired work on the Classics had produced several capacious volumes on Greek Particles.

Aunt Mary held famous Sunday Lunches, still legendary among those privileged to have attended them, mainly the young – students who had stayed in her house and now moved on, present students, writers, nieces, artists, musicians. Large proof-copies of world maps served as tablecloths. Aunt Mary had been employed by the Cartography Department of the University to edit these. While eating one could trace one's route along the Silk Road from Mongolia to Kathmandu, from China to Persia. Whenever I was off-duty, I was drawn there for the excellent company and fun.

A Greek quotation decorated part of a bedroom that, with the mere addition of a curtain and some elementary plumbing, had been turned into a bathroom. "Man rises from his bath-tub like the gods, the Immortals," my father translated from the hieroglyphics I copied out for him.

The house was Edwardian in its furnishings and lacked anything approaching modernity. Heating was supplied by one-bar electric fires. But the warmth of the welcome and the huge amount of food provided for the impecunious guests more than made up for the fact that gloves had to be worn most of the time to prevent frostbite. (Years later, when she was very old, Aunt Mary decided to remain 'independently' in her own house. We reckoned that, what with nieces and nephews, cousins, friends, official carers, meals-on-wheels, cleaners, doctors and district nurses – about thirty people contributed weekly to Aunt Mary's 'independence'.)

One day David said, "I think we'll go and buy a ring." There was no romantic nonsense about getting down on one knee and asking me to marry him, so I wasn't quite sure if I was engaged or not. It turned out I was. The Korean War had just broken out and David's immediate future was uncertain so we decided on an August wedding after he had returned from the Baltic with the Navy. Much to the annoyance of the midwifery authorities at the Radcliffe, I withdrew from Part Two of the course. (The so-called Third Part was DIY, having a baby oneself. This hadn't then entered my head.)

I had known David for less than six months and for much of this time he had been away at sea. This seems, from a twenty-twenty, sixty-year hindsight, an astonishingly short time to spend before embarking on such a momentous life-journey. Couples nowadays would probably live together for some years, 'practising for long enough', as Prince Charles remarked on Prince William's engagement to Kate, before a permanent commitment. But the same hindsight looks back on a forty-one year marriage which, like almost every one else's, had its minor ups and downs and was possibly not quite as perfect as youth and naivety had envisaged, but was as happy and quarrel-free, as mutually supportive and loving, as interesting in its work and travels and as productive (with a great deal of luck and a smidgen of good management) of charming and much loved children, as any human being could have wished.

Uncle Ed, the Bishop, officiated at our wedding, which took place in August 1950. It was only eleven months after that of my elder sister Diana, who, in keeping with a long clerical family tradition, married Peter Casswell who was about to be ordained. A year after my wedding, Camilla married Michael Francis, a stockbroker. At the end of all this, sighs of relief could be heard from our parents whose finances, after expensive ceremonies three years running, had suffered a severe shock.

"I have acquired in my sons-in-law," Rio remarked dryly, "a clergyman to rescue my soul, a financier to retrieve what is left of my investments and a sailor to protect my country."

12

The Morgan Family

I have often thought of the Morgans as being part of the professional backbone and 'salt of the earth' of Middle Britain in the nineteenth and through the twentieth centuries – at the same time both extraordinary and unexceptional. Their origins lay in the Welsh valleys and one family member, delving into mediaeval records, alleged that Hereward the Wake (or even, possibly, King Alfred) was a forebear. This was booted into touch by John Morgan who pronounced that it was 'complete rubbish'.

There was a Theophilus Morgan of Llantarnam, in South Wales, so far undated, possibly connected with the Morgans of Tredegar. (The crest on signet-rings worn to this day by male Morgans is that of the Tredegar family.) Walter Morgan was followed by his son John (1784–1832). His grandson, James Arthur Morgan, born in 1818, was a solicitor with various failed enterprises to his name. He wrote a book called *Reminiscences of a Grandfather* which, though somewhat tedious towards the end (being nothing more than a daily recital of plays seen, concerts heard, friends visited or received and short journeys undertaken) has been a most useful source of family dates and an insight into the life of a gentle, cultured and loving *pater familias*. He was musical from an early age and it was he who bought the Amati violin in 1840 for £50, which remained in the family for a hundred and fifty years.

An excerpt from James Arthur Morgan's book reads:

We visited Loudwater Church (Buckinghamshire) on 3rd May 1892... We also called the same day on Mr Pelly... In the afternoon (of 9th May) Mr and Miss Pelly called and were very pleasant... On 12th May, we called on the Pellys and had tea with them. Mrs Pelly was too ill to see us.

(See Pelly family tree, though I have not discovered where this Mr Pelly fits in – possibly he is a grandson of Sir John Henry Pelly.) From this, it was intriguing to discover that David's great-grandfather had met, on three occasions, a relative of mine, fifty-eight years before David and I encountered each other.

James Arthur's son, Joseph John Morgan, known as JJ, married, consecutively, two first cousins whose mothers, the Misses Twining, were sisters. The first marriage, in 1876, to Gertrude Croke Rowden, produced two sons and two daughters but his wife died while the four children were still very young.

He then married, in 1887, her first cousin Adelaide Holberton (raising sniffs of disapproval from those who thought the new marriage was undertaken rather too soon after his first wife's death) and had two more sons and another daughter. The two lots of children were therefore not only half-siblings but second cousins.

Nicknames flourished. Their father was called Fee. He seems to have been a most loving and gentle parent, administering none of the fierce discipline usually said to have been meted out by most Victorian fathers. Indeed, his youngest daughter, Mary, recalled sitting on her father's knee as a very small girl after she had committed some misdemeanour, while they both wept copiously – she for having sinned and he for having to correct her.

The First Lot

Arthur, nicknamed Bip, who was born in 1878 and was a solicitor in the firm, Park Nelson in London (used by Morgans for many years), became President of the Law Society and was eventually knighted. He was living in Winchester by the time I came on the scene. There is a story of him being visited by an old friend bearing a bottle of the very best claret. "Oh, Bip, dear old boy, I took the liberty of charging this bottle to your account and thought we could enjoy it together. Do you by any chance have any of those wonderful cigars left?"

In his youth, Bip had been among the first pupils at the then newly opened prep school, Horris Hill, just south of Newbury. Other Morgans followed him there – half-brothers Vaughan and Ed, David in the next generation and Nick and Simon in the following one.

Bip's first wife died in childbirth, producing his only son, John Arthur Theodore. A second marriage gave him three daughters, Ann (who married John Forest) and two known always by their nicknames – Mary (married to Paul Hildesley) was called 'Dobs' and Penelope (whose husband was John Allington) was 'Neps'. John served with much distinction during the Second World War in a sort of private army named 'Phantom' which moved, mysteriously and extremely bravely, behind enemy lines collecting information for the Allies. He was awarded the MBE for this work.

John sounds, from the accounts of other family members, to have been the ideal uncle – hospitable, generous, witty, wise and fun. After the war he became a publisher. He married Kay Smith late in life and had no children. His half-sisters had lots; Edward and Tom Forest, twins Christopher and Richard (known as Riche) and their brother Michael Hildersley, and Elizabeth, Giles, Katharine and Jane Allington.

Sybil, born in 1879 was better known as Aunt Syb. She trained as a nurse and worked with a friend in India delivering babies and dealing with tiger bites before becoming a nun in the enclosed Anglican Benedictine Abbey of West Malling. In spite of her incarceration behind bars she was one of the 'hubs' of the Morgans. Family news came spinning into the Abbey and out it went again to all the members. Visits were allowed and if you were under ten, you were permitted to penetrate the mysteries behind the barrier. Any older and kisses had to be exchanged and hands held between the upright railings.

Syb's face, framed by her white head-dress, had the unlined peacefulness of a truly good and loving person. She was passionately interested in the doings of the young of the family and followed their careers and the ups and downs of their lives with prayerful concern.

Cicely (Aunt Kit), who never married, worked for the Society for the Propagation of the Gospel, in which her brother Ed, the future Bishop, was also involved. She was a wonderfully eccentric character and left behind her, not only umbrellas and numerous string bags containing her possessions on almost every coach on which she frequently travelled, but also a series of *bons mots* known as 'Kitticisms', references to which are made to this day when family members congregate.

She was a shrewd and fearless judge of people. Seeing with great clarity through any insincerity or hypocrisy, she would sum up anyone showing signs of these failings with the scornful epithet, 'Rather a poor potato'.

One of the best of these Kitticisms occurred when, on holiday with the family, she was endeavouring to teach several young relations the art of surfing off a Cornish beach. (Where she had acquired such a skill has been lost in the inscrutability of time.)

One can imagine her standing on the beach, hair blown by the wind, in her shapeless black bathing-dress, issuing instructions. (Her 'fabulous legs' were remembered many years later by Hugh, a teenager at the time and a great-nephew.)

She shouts from the beach. "Look out, John, get ready – there's a wonderful one coming."

John looks back, like the biblical Mrs Lot turning to gaze at Sodom, and promptly falls off the board into the salty sea and the chaos of the breaking wave.

Kit's exasperated and much quoted exclamation bursts forth, "Oh, John, what a wicked waste of a wave!"

The youngest of the first lot was *Richard* who served throughout the First World War in the Royal Welsh Fusiliers but died in the global Spanish flu epidemic of 1919. He had two sons, Mike and Dick, neither of whom had children. His widow remarried later and had at least two more sons, one of whom, Neville Giradeau, considered himself an honorary Morgan in later life and became a friend of mine when he looked after the financial affairs of Sylvia, his half-brother Dick's widow. I was the executor of her Will and we used to meet at her Nursing Home in Winchester and have jolly lunches. Sylvia in her wheelchair and Geoffrey and I went to Paris, memorably, but that is a later story.

The Second Lot

Edmund (known as Uncle Ed). He was a truly saintly human being without being sanctimonious in any way, and was a loving and much loved parish priest, husband and father. He became the Principal of the College of the Ascension in Selly

Oak. (In his *Biography*, in a photograph dating from his time at the College, there is a woman standing beside him called Betty Tosh. In another extraordinary connection between my family and the Morgans, long before I met David, she was a first cousin of my mother, their mothers having been sisters. I had known her well as a child. She was the first person to call me 'Stephie' and get away with it – due only to my well-brought-up respect for my elders.)

Uncle Ed went on to become the Vicar and Archdeacon of Old Alresford, Suffragan Bishop of Southampton and finally Diocesan Bishop of Truro.

He was married to Isobel Charlotte née Jupp, known as Aunt Blue, a superbly unconventional woman, who was once reputed to have dried off a rain-soaked and chilly visiting Nigerian priest by putting him in the airing cupboard. Another tale is of her washing the kitchen floor with only an apron as a lower garment and, as a result, having to walk backwards ahead of an unexpected guest for fear of being seen from the back in her knickers. On another occasion, in need of a hat to attend a garden party, she appeared with her head adorned with a tea-cosy, the first thing that came to hand, without the slightest self-consciousness. Not altogether, one might think, in the usual run of Bishops' wives but a wise, supportive and much loved one.

When the family were living in Selly Oak (their Aunt Mary recalled later) the two elder sons, Hugh and Robert, aged six and nearly five, were asked one morning to bring an interesting object to school. They returned triumphantly in the afternoon bringing their little brother, Geoffrey, slightly bewildered, aged three.

The loss in the war of Hugh and Robert, and the severe wounding of Geoffrey, must have been devastating and almost unbearable misfortunes to Ed and Blue. Somehow, through the deep faith which sustained them even in the midst of such devastating tragedies, they managed the rest of their lives in an amazingly tranquil and serene manner.

Vaughan. This is my lovely father-in-law, the youngest boy of the family. After Horris Hill Prep School, he was sent off at thirteen to Osborne Naval College on the Isle of Wight, thence to Dartmouth in Devon and almost straight into the First World War. (His son, David, was similarly spewed into the beginning of the Second World War immediately on leaving Dartmouth.) Vaughan was Flag Lieutenant to Admiral Jellicoe at the Battle of Jutland which must have been exciting, and later the Admiral became godfather to David. Another godfather was the then Captain Dreyer – later an Admiral himself. They were all in New Zealand at the time of David's birth, on a round-the-world victory tour after the end of the First World War in 1919. On hearing the news of his son's safe arrival but being extremely busy, Vaughan asked Desmond Dreyer to send a telegram to Molly, his wife.

My future father-in-law had, in deference partly, it seems, to the long-vanished Welsh past of the family and partly after a younger brother of his father, been christened Llewellyn Vaughan, but never, ever, used his first name. (Indeed, many years later, when Vaughan was in Buckingham Palace, on the extreme verge of being dubbed 'Sir Llewellyn', Molly was heard to state, loudly and volubly, that there would be a divorce in the family if she found herself the wife of such a personage. Palace officials blanched visibly at this frightful wrecking of protocol, but managed to change the name just in time for the King to avert a marital split.)

Desmond Dreyer sent off a telegram as requested. This was read by an astonished Molly, lying in bed with her new-born son in his cot beside her. It said, 'Heartiest congratulations, Llewellyn.'

Working at the Admiralty some time between the wars,

Vaughan perched in London with his sister, Kit. She employed a beloved 'daily' who, probably all too easily, had avoided learning to read or write and who one day brought in her son's school report to be read. "Lovely words, I'm sure," she is said to have commented. Vaughan read them. 'Well below the average in every subject' was the terse account of a term's work.

"How has so-and-so done in his or her A Levels?" someone may nowadays ask a parent. "Well below the average in every subject" is the phrase that often comes into play at this juncture, especially if the youngster under discussion has finished rather well.

"Lovely wedding, my dear fellow," Vaughan is reported as saying to David at our wedding reception, "but I must just tell you about my mower. It's not going at all well..." And details of the near demise of the machine followed at some length while guests queued up to shake hands. He was a Scout Commissioner in his retirement, sporting shorts and a tie with a toggle, to his own and the amusement of friends.

He was showing some visiting Bishop round his garden at Meon Place in Soberton, when the prelate enquired the name of a pink flower. Never a knowledgeable gardener – more a labouring handyman – V wracked his brains. He came up with the combined names of their two maids. (This must have been at a time, possibly pre-war, when it was thought possible and affordable to have two such maids.)

"Oh, that's an Annie Saria," he announced confidently.

"Of course it is," replied the Bishop and they made their way back to the house for tea.

Mary Grace (MG) was the baby of the family and the only one of the three girls to marry. Extremely intelligent in a typically North Oxford way, she became the wife of the even more intellectual John Dewar Denniston known as 'Denny'.

He had the logical mind of a true classicist which was put to very good use in the Second World War for interrogating spies. Train journeys to London to carry out this work were enlivened by games of chess in the train. He was the author of the previously mentioned highly praised volumes on the subject of Greek Particles. They had no children.

13

Libby, David and Prue

When their children were young my future in-laws lived in Victoria Road, Kensington and as a small boy David was taken for walks in the Gardens by the nanny. "If only you *knew* how tired I am you wouldn't make me walk so far," he would complain, dragging along behind the pram containing the infant Prue. Every now and then, however, his father suggested sailing a boat on the Round Pond. The change in David was immediate and dramatic. Displaying not a hint of tiredness, he would dart about getting ready and then run beside his striding, boat-carrying father, urging him on to greater speed.

His mother took him to his first school in Sloane Street on the back of her bicycle. When he was a little older she would see off this diminutive small boy, in his grey shorts and red cap, as he bravely caught a bus and took himself off to school. No parent nowadays would dare to allow such a solitary journey.

Later, David boarded at Horris Hill Prep School where occasionally, on a Sunday, his parents visited and attended the compulsory Church service. To a small boy, the embarrassment and discomfiture caused by his mother wearing galoshes was further compounded by his father intoning "Amen", very loudly *after* the rest of the congregation.

At thirteen he was sent to Dartmouth Naval College, following in his father's wake. He was not an outward-bounding, sporty child and his time there was miserable. The discipline was harsh and the narrow education which had, of course, much to do with the Navy, left little room for the gentler humanities, literature or art. In later life, his quite frequent nightmare involved arriving to take part in some high-powered occasion and discovering that he was without some vital piece of uniform, or had brown shoes instead of black or had mislaid his tie or medals.

David was born in 1919, his birth timed perfectly (if that's the right word) to be flung into the Second World War at the age of just twenty. Most of the war he spent dangerously at sea including the Atlantic Convoys. The book, *The Cruel Sea*, by Nicholas Montserrat, tells the vivid story of these convoys and the horrors of the intense cold of the open bridge, the dark ocean heaving with incipient seasickness, the constant danger from the U-boats and the exhaustion of working four hours on, four hours off, round the clock. Taking leave for a day or two in Liverpool between voyages was the only respite.

Another of his ships was bombed in dry dock in Grand Harbour, Malta, and he was awarded the MBE for bravery and for saving a friend from bleeding to death. He had to return home via neutral Portugal and Ireland, briefly enjoying their comparatively better food and bright lights.

His father was also mainly afloat in command of ships. Molly, his mother, formidable though she was, must have had even her strength tested with anxiety, not only for her husband and son, but for both her daughters as well. The younger one, Prue, had caught polio at school at Sherborne when she was seventeen and had been treated in Oxford. She partially recovered, but was to get about on crutches for most of the rest of her life.

When Michael Le Fanu, a young naval officer came

calling at Meon Place in the late Forties, Prue assumed that he was there to pay court to Libby, her beautiful elder sister. No-one would be interested in her, she thought, because of her disability. When he asked her to marry him, she was astonished. She had discounted all the qualities that Michael had seen in her – great intelligence, wit, courage and calmness in adversity.

She stumped down the aisle on crutches for her wedding and followed the life of a naval wife as normally as any other. "Yes, of course," she would say to any suggestion of adventure or distant or difficult travel – and only then would she and Michael sort out the complications involved. He carried her onto many a ship and when she stayed with us in Orkney she was 'craned' in a bosun's chair onto the ferry to the island of Hoy with no sign of nerves.

Michael was the Commander-in-Chief Middle East in the late Sixties and they were stationed in Aden. I had my first (and only) flight in a helicopter when I visited them, hovering over the huddled houses and narrow streets and seeing the background of mountains and the waters of the Gulf of Aden. He was a magnificent walker and I climbed with him, twice, in boiling heat, up a nearby mountain feeling intrepid, very hot and, by the time we arrived back, exhausted.

We all flew in his military aircraft on an official visit to Kenya, to stay with the British High Commissioner in Nairobi. Everyone was extremely brainy and witty and the evenings were spent tossing off *The Times* crossword in double quick time. If I could contribute even a single word before anyone else drawled it out with languid ease, I felt enormously elated.

From Nairobi we drove up between the high hills of the Rift Valley to Lake Nakuru National Park to see the enormous flocks of flamingos, possibly between one and two million of them. They turned the whole lake pink as they stalked about on their absurdly long legs and fed in the brackish water.

In 1969, when David and I had been in Singapore for a year, Michael came on an official visit and stayed with us in the Naval Base. Most uncharacteristically, he asked if he could lie down in the afternoon as he was feeling tired. Tired? Michael? It was unheard of. And anyway he was due to become the Chief of the General Staff – the most senior member of the British Armed Forces – later that year and couldn't possibly be ill.

He died, however, of leukaemia in November 1970 without being able to take up this post and his memorial service was held, memorably, in Westminster Abbey. I have an unprovable and quite possibly incorrect theory that, after the end of the war when he was in the Far East, at the time when atomic explosions were being tested and when people watching these were merely told to put on dark glasses as a mild precaution against the glare, he might have been affected by the radiation and contracted the disease.

Prue moved down to South Harting after Michael's death and it was good to have her so near to us. When she became ill one Sunday morning, I dashed round and phoned the local doctor who was a friend and who came to see her.

"I'm afraid you've had a stroke, Prue," he said as gently as possible.

There was a slight pause. "Oh, bother," said Prue crossly and was whisked off to Haslar hospital, where she died a few days later.

Prue's elder sister Libby gave their parents grounds for a different concern altogether from Prue's polio. One of her godmothers had converted to Catholicism in later life and had prevailed on a willing Libby to do the same. This was totally anathema to Molly. (I once overheard a man at a cocktail party spit out the words, "I would rather my daughter married a black man than a Catholic.") This possible conversion produced many damaging and ongoing arguments and disputes between mother and daughter, causing Libby to have a mental breakdown. She suffered the archaic operation of pre-frontal leucotomy from which she emerged with a large gap in her memory, recalling only that she wished still, after all that, to be a Catholic.

She was a great beauty in her youth. Geoffrey Morgan told me much later that his status at his school, Bloxhams, near Oxford had risen astronomically when she came to visit him, her younger first cousin. Many of the older boys jostled to be introduced to her and Geoffrey bathed in reflected glory. During the early part of the war, she became engaged to the headmaster of Wellington, only to hear that he had been killed by a stray bomb on his own playing field. Other romances followed, each ending in some tragic way.

When Libby at last found someone to love, the fact that he had been married during the war, for no longer than a weekend, to an Italian woman who would now not cooperate with having the marriage annulled, meant that, being a Catholic, Libby could not marry him. Perhaps converts then were stricter with the rules of their religion than many a cradle-Catholic is now, but it is an example of the way in which what could have been a last hope of happiness was blighted by a man-made set of Church laws. She became a teacher of small children, continued as a devoted Catholic – her house in London piled high with many years of dusty issues of *The Tablet* – and managed her life remarkably well in spite of these troubles, with only one more severe lapse, much later, into mental difficulties.

When I was being taken, quaking inwardly, by David, for a first inspection by his parents, we called in at Prue and Michael Le Fanu's house in Petersfield on the way. She had produced, at that time, two small children: Mark, aged three, and Victoria, (always called Toy) aged eighteen months. Mark was reported to have asked later while saying his prayers, "And God bless the lady wot Uncle David bringed." David told me, much later, that Prue had said of me, "This is the one, dear Bro. Go for it!"

(David had been engaged earlier to Joanna Allen, an arrangement that was broken off. Years later, after his father had long retired and recently been widowed by Molly's death, Vaughan had married Eirene Allen, Joanna's mother, herself the widow of a naval Captain. By marrying again, this time to a retired officer, Eirene forfeited her naval pension and when Vaughan himself died she was not eligible for even a third of his pension. The Treasury thus saved itself the cost of any allowance for the widow of two distinguished naval officers and left Eirene without an income. It was only by the strenuous efforts of Airey Neave MP – later blown up and killed in his car by the IRA as he was leaving the Palace of Westminster – that a measly two thousand pounds a year was squeezed from a reluctant Treasury.)

14

Early Married Life

The Morgans lived in Meon Place in Soberton, a house looking down across the garden to the valley of the River Meon and the about-to-be-closed railway line from Alton to Fareham. Sir Vaughan Morgan (known as Pom by his grandchildren) had only recently retired from being Admiral Superintendent of Portsmouth Dockyard. Here Lady M had been in her element as the Admiral's wife, with plenty of staff to do her bidding. Now she was reduced to a single maid called Phyllis.

Phyllis had committed some minor misdemeanour and thought she had covered her tracks. She was sent for and confronted with the Awful Truth.

"How did you know about it, m'Lady?" Phyllis asked tremulously.

"Phyllis," replied Molly loftily, "I know *everything*."

No girl, short, just possibly, of the daughter of a belted earl, was ever going to be good enough for Molly's only son, of course, but she was welcoming and hospitable in a guarded way. Vaughan was warm and amusing and gathered me into the family so that the nervousness of meeting the possible in-laws quickly faded in fun and laughter.

A 'bed-sit with bath and kit' at the top of a house in

Pembroke Square in London which belonged to a couple of friends was ample accommodation for the first six months of married life, while David attended a course at Greenwich. These friends had sent us a wedding present of a fully equipped picnic basket. On opening it we came across a card saying, 'To David and Stephanie, with love from Peter and Rosemary'. Delving a little deeper, we found another gift tag. It said 'To Peter and Rosemary, with love from Joan and Graham'. I think we too passed it on but were particularly careful to remove both cards.

We then found a flat in the wrong part of West Hampstead for £5 a week, two floors up, just off the Finchley Road. I went back to King's for Nick to be born, testing the place out for the second time as patient rather than staff. Fathers didn't, in those days, feel it necessary to be present at the arrival of their young, so, having driven me in, David went home, got on with his knitting – he was making an extremely small cardigan in some intricate stitch, so diminutive that it fitted the new baby for about a week (I have it still) and had a good night's sleep.

I was in awe of Molly for some time. It was soon after Nick was born and we were staying at Meon Place for me to recuperate, that I was brave enough to stand up to her.

"You'll have Nicholas circumcised, of course," she remarked authoritatively one morning. I was still in my dressing gown, which put me at a disadvantage when addressing my well-dressed and manicured mother-in-law. Fresh from my nursing training, however, when no operation was ever undertaken unless entirely necessary, I felt like a tiger defending her cub.

"I will take him to the doctor," I said firmly. "If he needs to be circumcised he will be. If not, he won't." And I did and he didn't.

My mother-in-law began to think it was possible that

there was more to respect of me than met the eye. Years later, when I had had some minor triumph approved of by her, Prue's husband, Michael, by then an Admiral himself, sent me one of many typical postcards. 'WTMWTWC!' it said cryptically. The translation, in small letters underneath, read 'Welcome To Molly's Whiter Than White Club!' He was, of course, already in it himself.

As Nick grew heavier, heaving him up two floors to the flat got strenuous. Molly found us part of a large house on the edge of Swanmore which was divided into five variously sized units. It was not far away from them at Soberton and we moved in 1952, when Nick was about six months old, to Swanmore House, near Bishop's Waltham.

David continued to work in Whitehall and perched with my parents in Wimbledon during the week. It was there that my father passed on to him his addiction to the hardest possible crosswords, those in *The Listener*. This obsession lasted them for the rest of their lives and both won several prizes which spurred them on.

Early in 1955, Molly and Vaughan dashed over in their ancient Austin 10 one day, bursting with pride. "David has been promoted to Commander!" they announced with forgivable satisfaction. Michael had heard the news early and phoned his in-laws.

Charlotte was born while David was away on duty in Scotland. We had just sold our part of Swanmore House, preparatory to David's next appointment and I was staying, together with young Nick and a temporary nanny, with my in-laws at Meon Place. I woke them in the night to ask them to take me to the Maternity Home in Shawford. We dawdled through the dark country roads. "Would it be possible to go a bit faster, Pom?" I enquired politely of my father-in-law, as waves of contractions swept over me.

"I've left my glasses at home, darling," he confessed,

"but I'll speed up as much as I can."

In spite of his comparative blindness, we arrived safely. The midwives were Plymouth Brethren and, if anything went wrong, were apt to gather together and fall on their knees in prayer. Regular praying sessions were held as well, even if nothing was going amiss, leaving the patient to get on with her contractions alone. I found this prospect disconcerting but fortunately Charlotte arrived without the need of divine intervention – the first grand-daughter for my parents after three grandsons. (They eventually acquired sixteen, eleven boys and five girls.) A fellow newly-delivered mother had just produced her fourth son and was green with envy of my luscious daughter. We lay about on the floor, doing our post-natal exercises and laughed so much that we were in danger of disturbing the entire building and the praying midwives.

We were required to stay in for two weeks and a very great boredom set in once my new friend had been allowed to escape. She was replaced by a singularly tedious and rather elderly woman who had produced, apparently somewhat to her surprise, what was clearly to be her very-late-in-life only child. I longed to break out from my enforced idleness.

There is now a considerable difference. People are sent home within hours of giving birth. Perhaps a happy compromise could be arrived at, say, forty-eight hours rest before rejoining the busy world.

15

Scapa Flow

Charlotte was five weeks old and Nick was three and a half when David's appointment as Resident Naval Officer (RNO) Orkney, began. Such was my ignorance that I had to look the place up on a map and found it squashed, with its cousin Shetland, into the Moray Firth in a little square on its own, the cartographer having run out of space at the top of the page.

Before we left, David met a friend – an ambitious and clever fellow officer – as they waited for a train on the Underground.

"On leave?" enquired Edward. "What are you doing next?"

"RNO Orkney, Scapa Flow," replied David.

"My dear fellow," cried a shocked Edward. "What *have* you done to deserve that? It's the back of beyond and will do frightful damage to your career. I wouldn't have considered it for one moment."

"Well, I've agreed to go there," said David. "I've heard the fishing is very good."

Edward sighed, the train came in and he went on, much later, to become First Sea Lord. David also had a perfectly respectable, distinguished and successful career.

David travelled to Orkney ahead of us. Nick, Charlotte and I took the sleeper train to Aberdeen, where I deposited the slumbering Charlotte in the Left Luggage Office in her carry-cot, while Nick and I ate a hearty breakfast in the station café.

In the plane to the Mainland Island of Orkney from Aberdeen, Nick brought up his hearty breakfast neatly into a paper bag and a man sitting nearby kindly offered to hold Charlotte while I dealt with this. "I have a baby girl of my own," he said, handling her expertly and gazing at her in a besotted fashion. I didn't get her back till we landed in Kirkwall.

The long Nissen hut on the island of Hoy, in part of which we lived, had been the Mess in the days when Lyness had been an important naval base. To the east it looked over abandoned small fields, out to the distant islands of Flotta and Cava and the grey heaving waters of Scapa Flow. Beneath these lay the remains of HMS *Royal Oak,* torpedoed six weeks into the war by a single German submarine and now an official War Grave. To the west, bleak, undulating moorland was dotted with windswept hummocks of heather and cotton grass. Further west was Ward Hill, one of the only two hills that Orkney possesses and, just offshore, the tall sea-battered pillar of the Old Man of Hoy.

Half a ton of coal arrived weekly for cooking and heating. Several geese seemed to be part of the establishment and the three-year-old Nick bustled into their enclosure in his little gumboots without apparent fear of their hissing beaks and lowered necks. I took him down to the only shop one day.

"What can I do for you, Nicholas?" asked the kindly shop owner, leaning over the counter and smiling.

"I'm not going to tell you," was his unusually grumpy reply and out he stumped. Julia and I laughed and agreed that it was a curious way of going shopping. I bowled Charlotte back in her pram, singing "Little Charlotte Morgan is the only girl for me", to the tune of *The Rose of Texas* – the sound swept away on the howling gale. Nick trailed along behind, scuffing his boots in the mud. It was clearly an off day.

No television existed at that time so the inhabitants of the Base provided their own entertainments. Scottish Country dancing to the sound of recorded bagpipes was popular and warming. An occasional film and monthly play-reading provided opportunities for over-acting and a few histrionics. Bingo was another innocent diversion. I headed a team of women footballers on one memorable occasion during which we cheated a great deal by handling the ball, to loud shouts of protest from our male opponents, whenever it seemed beneficial to our side to do so. (After all they do it in rugby matches.) The game was abandoned quite early due to exhaustion, and both sides retired to the hut which served as a community centre for restorative drinks.

I had known so little about life on the islands before arriving that I wrote to Woman's Hour, suggesting that they broadcast a programme from there. Other people might possibly be as ignorant as I had been. The BBC agreed and came up to Kirkwall. Many engaging local folk were interviewed and we heard about the great Cathedral of St Magnus, the beautiful Italian chapel made by prisoners of war on the small island of Lamb Holm and ancient sites like Skara Brae and the Standing Stones of the Islands. I was invited to take part with a six minute script. They paid me five pounds for this, much to David's chagrin. He had spent hours and much brain-power making up extremely difficult crosswords for *The Listener* and they paid him the measly sum of three pounds, ten shillings each.

Part of the reason for David's acceptance of the appointment had been his love of fishing. He went off in the ferry to the Mainland Island to one of the many trout-filled lochs among the Standing Stones and returned in the evening tired and happy.

"Did you have a good day?" I asked.

"Wonderful," he replied.

"Where are the fish then?"

"Oh, I didn't *catch* anything," replied the true fisherman. "It was still a wonderful day."

(David and his father had fished in Benbecula in the Outer Hebrides on many occasions and once, after a happy week, made their way back to the quay, battling through a major gale. The harbourmaster leant into the wind, scanning the heaving sea. There was no sign of the expected ferry which was of to take them back to the mainland.

"What are the chances of her being able to sail, harbourmaster?" they bawled above the storm, anxious about their return on time to their work.

"That depends on God and Captain MacLean," he shouted into the wind, "and they're two good men.")

Lady Skrine, whose husband Sir Claremont appeared briefly from time to time, lived, along with thirty or so cats, in an isolated house halfway up the only road north from the naval base. The children and I were invited to tea on several occasions. With difficulty, I headed off Nick's comments on the smell of the place, as felines swarmed round our legs and scratched at the already shredded furnishings. Lady S waded through the purring throng carrying the tea tray before dislodging a cat or two from her armchair and settling down with several on her lap. I think we were her only visitors, unsurprisingly.

Mac Stewart, middle aged, rich, divorced and lonely, lived during the summer months in Hoy Lodge, at the north-west end of the road. This looked out over the narrow Hoy Sound to the town of Stromness on the Mainland Island.

He and Lady S did not speak, for some long forgotten but smouldering reason. They might have been termed the only relatively permanent incomers on the island. Fortunately we were kindly accepted by both and Mac later took to visiting us in far-flung corners of the globe.

HMS *Virago* arrived, flying the Admiral's flag and anchored in the middle of Scapa Flow. We were invited to dinner on board. In spite of the radio informing us that the gale warning was no longer in operation, the storm continued to shriek round, under and over the house, rattling every door and ill-fitting window. The dinner was cancelled. David and I stood dejectedly sipping our own gin in our own drawing room, dressed in our best clothes.

Earlier, sixty-six sailors had come ashore for a football match and a dance. It was impossible to get them back to the ship so they all had to be found accommodation. David abandoned the gin and disappeared into the noisy night. I answered some of the numerous telephone calls dripping coldly on to the Admiralty linoleum, leaving the bath, taken rashly in a quiet moment, to do so.

The coastguards rang, Wick radio rang, ship owners and agents rang, Rosyth rang, the wireless office rang – and rang.

David had still not returned when the secretary of the Lifeboat Committee phoned at midnight. A coaster was in trouble in the Pentland Firth and the Longhope lifeboat was about to leave. "Could the Commander, in his capacity as honorary stern-sheet-man, just slip along the ten miles of winding road and join the outing?" I was afraid it was unlikely – he had other pressing duties on hand.

Wind-blown, he returned at three am, took off his top layer of clothes and was up again at five. At seven, we drove down to the beach, taking a horribly bright and breezy small boy with us, to see the drifter, which had at last taken the men back to the ship, returning empty. HMS *Virago* steamed slowly away. It had been an interesting night.

The lifeboat station at Longhope had been established in 1874. Eighty-one years later, when we were there, the famous Dan Kirkpatrick was the Coxswain who, during his long service, received a Bronze medal, a Silver Medal for the rescue of nine men from a trawler, another Silver for the rescue of fifteen crewmen from a further trawler, plus a extra award for the same incident, for the bravest act of life-saving. In March 1969 the worst tragedy in British Lifeboat history occurred when Dan and two of his sons, together with the other five crew members, were all lost at sea when answering a Mayday call during one of the most severe storms in the islands. There is a memorial to them all in Kirkhope cemetery, near the lifeboat station.

At the beginning of our stay in Hoy many people asked me how I was enjoying being there. With two very small children, far from the supportive back-up of family and friends, on a distant island almost as far away from familiar surroundings as the British Isles allow, I lied through gritted teeth that it was lovely and I liked it very much. By the time we left sixteen months later, I really loved the wildness, the closeness of the sea, the comparative isolation and the friendly people. I wished we could stay. As we drove through Kirkwall to the airport, the bells of the town were doing their best to deafen the population. Clearly this was the proper way to see us off and to mark our sixth wedding anniversary. The observance of the Queen Mother's birthday may have shared in the salutations.

16

Malta

We arrived in Malta, exchanging one island for another, as the Suez crisis was looming and humiliation at the hands of the Americans was imminent. It was the autumn of 1956. David joined the HQ, Allied Forces, Mediterranean (HAFMED) in Valletta. It was made up of Turkish, French, Italian, Greek, American and British officers, most with wives in tow.

Apart from the Americans and British, the wives varied greatly in their command of the English tongue, as we did in theirs. I called it 'grinning in six languages'. Some gave demonstrations of their native cooking – I still harbour my revulsion at the garlic snails, lovingly prepared by the French, as my teeth bounced off these rubbery little horrors.

Our home was in the oldest part of Malta – the walled hill-top city of Mdina. The ancient house, on the corner of Villegaignon Street and Bastion Square, looked east over the parapet down to St Paul's Bay. The thick stone walls cooled us in summer and chilled us in winter. Good Friday was the only day of the year free from the sound of bells at all hours. Across a valley on the next hill, the military hospital of Imtarfa was conveniently close for fairly frequent visits. Cut knees, unexpected rashes, vaccinations, and most importantly, Simon's birth in December 1957, took us up onto the neighbouring hill.

Both Nick and Charlotte chose this time to have measles.

Being pregnant was helpful when trying to converse with languagely-challenged Turkish ladies. There was much smiling and gesturing to the 'bump'. It was not so beneficial when my mother-in-law came to stay. The October thunderstorms raged for three nights on Molly's arrival. These culminated in several inches of water on the ground floor. I was 'huge and hot and lumbering', as Prue inelegantly described pregnancy, and I had had one of those haircuts that can only be termed 'unfortunate'. When my own parents came on a visit, during a particularly cold and disappointing spring, the wind wailed round the house and crept in through every crevice. Orkney, for the most part, had been warmer.

No-one to do with the Forces was allowed to deliver their babies at home. It was over to the hospital at Imtarfa, where they were all produced with military precision, the new mothers sitting to attention in bed when the Commander-in-Chief's wife graciously visited the lower orders. Meanwhile, the *au pair* was nobly coping with double measles. (Three years later, Simon was a page boy, dressed as a very small and unreliable sailor, at the wedding of the same Commander-in-Chief's daughter when we were all stationed in Chatham.)

On summer Sundays, we took off early for the beach while it was still cool and breakfasted there. As later picnickers arrived mid-morning, we gathered up our three brown children and returned up the hill to the coolness of the house and the small walled garden. An ancient tortoise lived there and was serially inherited by each succeeding tenant.

Nick, aged seven, climbed the tree in the inner flagstone courtyard. "Shall I jump?" he enquired. "No," I replied firmly. But he did, catching a foot and landing on his head on the flags. There was yet another visit to Casualty for him, driven there, weeping, by a furious and far from sympathetic mother. "I *told* you not to jump."

A young maid called Jessie cleaned and tidied the house and generally took charge. She became one of the family and we exchanged Christmas cards annually ever after. Years later, now married, she named her daughter Stephanie. Nick, who had been eight years old when we left, visited the island with the Navy as a young doctor. He called on her unannounced.

She opened the door. Without a second's hesitation she exclaimed delightedly, "Nicholas!"

She died far too young and her husband continues the Christmas card tradition, giving news of their highly intelligent and successful offspring.

I decided to have roast duck as the main course for a dinner to which we had invited David's Admiral and the Captain, his immediate boss. It was not a good idea to have left the prepared ducks on top of the fridge overnight. The fridge itself, which ran on oil, had had a nasty turn and was emitting clouds of smoke. That the bottled gas had chosen this moment to run out was a further disaster. We had also omitted to close the doors of the integral garage that night and local cats had a most delicious supper of raw duck.

Roast duck, for some mad reason, it still had to be. I visited the local poultry farm, chose three ducks on the hoof, as it were, bore the bodies home and dealt with feathers and innards. They were, of course, virtually uneatable.

"I think the knives aren't very sharp," commented the Admiral kindly, refuting my embarrassed apologies.

Colin, also in the Navy, and Jill Lings became our great friends. They had no children and would make occasional disparaging comments about those of their friends who 'talked of nothing else but their young'. Years later, when we were all at home again, they adopted two children and became as obsessed about these as, no doubt, we had been earlier. Jill was one of the most life-enhancing friends I ever had and it was devastating when she eventually died, far too young, of malignant melanoma.

Near the end of David's appointment, the children, our French *au pair* and I sailed back to England in the troopship *Devonshire*. Having spent a few days at sea getting my sea-legs before reaching the turbulent Bay of Biscay, I was amazed not to be turning green, and even to be enjoying it, as the ship wallowed and heaved. At Southampton, no visitors were allowed to come on board before we disembarked, but I was not in the least surprised to see my in-laws mounting the gangway. Molly had ways of getting what she wanted, which in this case was to meet her latest grandson, the fifteen-month-old Simon, and it was useful to have a title and an Admiral for a husband.

It was May, and from the windows of the train taking us all back to London, the leaves on trees, the bushes and grass, seemed miraculously green after two and a half years of the sand-coloured landscape of Malta.

"I was a battered baby," Simon insists, enjoying a bout of entirely false gloom. I was not a battering mother but there was one occasion when I slipped up. In our house in Malta, at the end of the top landing there had been a dilapidated wooden door dividing us from a small flat. Behind this door lived a childless naval wife whose lifestyle differed considerably from ours. I couldn't allow Simon, as a young baby, to cry in the night – our neighbour had probably just turned in after a long and jolly evening. Simon had therefore acquired the habit, in the small hours, of notifying us, loudly, that he was awake and would like a change of pants and a cuddle. Blearily, I would get up and cater to his demands.

Back in England, on leave between appointments, we perched in my parents' holiday cottage in Pulborough. Simon was in a drop-side cot in my room. No-one was inconvenienced by his continued vociferous requirements except me. After several broken nights it was too much. I took my slipper and gave him a whack on his bottom, over several layers of nappy, pyjamas, blankets and eiderdown. There was an astonished silence. No further 'battering' was required, but Simon still enjoys his little joke.

17

The Great Snows

We relocated to Chatham – David was to be the Commander of the Barracks. There was then a naval hospital conveniently placed to receive, as before, our routine visits for such calamities as cut heads. Hugh, my sister-in-law Prue's youngest, much the same age as Nick, came to stay and both cousins suffered stitchable wounds after a bout of tile-throwing on the roof of a derelict building. And when Simon was about three, he came in from the garden one day with red smears all over his mouth.

"Eated strawberries," he announced by way of explanation. This seemed unlikely in September. We went out to look at the 'strawberries'. Woody Nightshade greeted us – not quite as poisonous as the Deadly kind but bad enough to require a stomach washout. I was banned from being present at this procedure and a somewhat despondent small boy was returned home next day.

Promotion in the Navy is well regulated. Officers are in the Zone (for promotion to Captain) for only eight years. David had been promoted to Commander relatively early, thereby entering the Zone fairly young. The years went by and he was on his 'last shot' in the summer of 1961. On the day of the publication of the promotions, unaware of the cliff-hanger situation, I had been idling at the hairdresser and returned home to receive a telephone message from David's Chief Petty Officer secretary. "*My* Commander has been promoted to Captain," he declared, pride cracking his voice, "*and* he's top of the List." (Every naval officer knows that whoever is 'top of the List' is almost certainly on his last shot and has been on tenterhooks as he awaits the news. David had heroically not involved me in his anxiety.)

A spell at the Admiralty followed for David. No married quarters were available in London so, with financial help from my father, we bought a suburban house in New Malden for the princely sum, then, of £7,000. We occupied this for a year before David's office moved from London to Bath. We let the house through an agent. Messages from fascinated former neighbours informed us that our house was now a brothel. The twitching curtains were agog. These tenants having been disposed of, it took five man-hours to clean the oven alone, not to mention other regions. Our affection for the place, never strong from the first, evaporated. The house was sold without hesitation or regret.

Friends had told us of a possible cottage to rent in the tiny hamlet of Woolley, in the country on the north-east rural outskirts of Bath. It was only just big enough for us but the views were wide and lovely over a valley and fields and hills, the friends lived just over the road and the greenness of the countryside after grey suburban streets was wonderful.

In the Domesday Book the village of Woolley was valued at sixty shillings and housed sixty-eight souls. Rising to the dizzy number of a hundred and four people in 1831, it had sunk back to sixty-one by the late twentieth century. In the 1750s there was a (Gun) Powder Mill down by the river Lam and in 1761 the great architect John Wood the Younger, having built the Royal Crescent, the Assembly Rooms and other grand structures in Bath, had turned his attention to Woolley Church.

This neglected Norman building was pulled down and the new classical-looking church built. It too had later needed much maintenance so the tiny village strenuously raised enough money for a fund to provide for present and future repairs and conservation.

The Great Snows occurred in the winter of 1962/63. Coming home from Bath in the bus from a pantomime soon after Christmas, we noticed the first large snow flakes drifting down from a leaden sky. Soon the hamlet was snowed in. David took lifts on a tractor to reach his work and the lanes were filled with snow to the top of the hedges. This hung about for many weeks. There was plenty of scope for tobogganing in the sloping fields, with our new puppy, Woolley, racing, in clouds of snowflakes, to keep up. He was a large-sized Peke who had been born across the road and grew up thinking he was a Labrador. The children took one look at the wriggling furry infant and decided immediately that he should join the family.

"You are a very nice, good little boy," I was heard saying to Simon one day by our neighbour, the 'mother' of Woolley, who had strolled across the road. (What had occasioned this approval I have long since forgotten.)

"Oh," she said, "I do like to hear a mother praising a child instead of shouting at it. Here's a bit of chocolate, Simon – I'm sure you deserve it."

Deserving or not, Simon was very pleased.

Events across the Atlantic occurred. The nerve-jangling tension of the Cuban crisis, with the USA and the Soviets playing deadly games of 'who blinks first', with the fate of world peace hanging yet again on the result, was chilling. The relief when Russia backed down was intense.

18

Boating and Butlins

We had made our way to Bath somewhat unconventionally, via a holiday in France. Leaving New Malden was no hardship. We crossed the Channel for a holiday in Normandy where, as usual, David joined us later and eventually left us all sitting on the quay in St Malo, the children weeping into their fish and chips, when he had to go home before us. In the meantime, we had visited Mont St Michel, where the tide comes in 'faster then a galloping horse', and, at the camp-site, Simon had refused to make use of the sanitary arrangements for a whole week, objecting both to the aroma and the squat-type facilities provided by the management. (When we all went later to Ireland, Simon was the only one of us who refused to kiss the Blarney Stone, asserting, aged about nine, probably correctly, that it was unhygienic.)

'No maggots are allowed on board this boat', announced a large notice on the wall of the canal-boat as we arrived for another holiday. We took, of course, no notice. How can one fish in canals without maggots? We had ventured no more than a nautical mile from the Base station when the boat required the attention of the Base engineer. He visited much too quickly, since the distance by road took a mere ten minutes. We had no wish to cause him distress and the maggots were hidden from view only just in time. After he had left, the vessel being once again in a viable state, we sat on the roof of the boat catching the occasional uneatable fish and listening on the radio to England winning the 1966 World Cup.

Bracken, the next dog, accompanied us on many a water-borne adventure, adding to the dramas by taking the unwise decision to leap from the boat as we moved under a bridge, failing to make landfall and descending into the fast-narrowing gap between the boat and the footpath wall. He was rescued from a certain and painful death in the nick of time. I leapt off the roof, where I had been attending to my nails in a leisurely way, scattering from my lap all the implements required for such an activitiy and hauled up the dripping dog by the scruff of his neck. He was not a quick learner and this was a far from unique occurrence.

There is a photo of a much loved later dog, Rum, a favourite black Labrador, standing under a large notice at one mooring point, which stated that no dogs were allowed ashore at that particular place. She was, of course, unable to read though otherwise endowed with all the excellent qualities of her breed. Daughter of Fruit, my nephew Nutty's dog, she inherited all her mother's superior characteristics and hardly put a paw wrong throughout her life.

One morning we woke to find the boat at a slight angle, sitting on the glossy mud of an unexpectedly waterless section of the canal. The authorities, when called on to comment on this turn of events, accused us of having left the previous lock-gates open. We refuted this strongly, and pointed out that both our lock-keys had been stolen during the night. Could the miscreants who had stolen these be responsible for the dehydrated state of the canal? Reluctantly, they agreed that this was a possible explanation for the aridity around us and set to work to get us floating again. Some hours later, buoyant once more and in possession of freshly purchased lock-keys, we continued our interrupted voyage.

Drifting along at the maximum permitted speed of four miles an hour, through quiet countryside unseen by those moving at greater velocity along busy motorways, we enjoyed the occasional contrast when passing, for example, under Spaghetti Junction in Birmingham, between our serene pace and the noisy overhead passage of busy cars, buses and lorries. The falling into the canal of various dogs and children and once, memorably, of their father, were about the only disturbers of our peaceful progress.

On another not altogether drama-free, two-boat/two-family, River Thames voyage from Maidenhead to Oxford one summer, Camilla's handbag fell off a shelf into the chemical lavatory, discharging its entire contents into the blue liquid at the bottom with predictably dire results. Neither she nor Michael were experts at steering their vessel so their morale, which had not been at its highest even before this happened, deteriorated further.

An embarrassing episode occurred when Nick, who had been put in charge of our boat when we tied up in a lock, decided to dash off for a pee just as the water began to drain away. By the time he returned the boat hung bow up, stern down, gently crushing the port bow against the lock wall. There was a lot of shouting and rushing about and the sound of wood-cracking. The rope was somehow released and the boat descended with a splash into the fast diminishing water. We slunk out to the sound of the lock-keeper's imprecations ringing in our ears.

The great naval Captain was obliged to report this incident to the firm of boat owners. "Hm... er, this is Mr Morgan. I'm sorry to have to tell you... "

Having run out of ideas for something new to eat on a camping holiday near St Jean de Luz, I had bought a tin of *Tripe à la Provençale*. 'The French are such good cooks', I reckoned, 'that even tinned tripe is bound to be delicious.' Full of hope, I served it up without divulging its identity.

"Ugh, what's this?" was the instant comment as it was pushed about on their plates. I confessed. We put it outside the tent for any passing dog to enjoy for a treat and were interested to observe the approach of several of these. All sniffed the snack questioningly and passed by on the other side.

"There, you see, Mum, even the dogs won't eat it." Suitably chastened, I have avoided this delicacy ever since.

During the last night of this otherwise sun-soaked week in south-west France, we cowered in our tent, avoiding the leaks, while persistent and heavy rain thundered onto the canvas. Simon slept throughout this ordeal but woke to wail, "There's a slug on my banana!" Peering out at the camp-site playground, we could see the seats of the swings floating on a couple of feet of water.

The sodden tent had little time to dry out and the car, filled with the five of us and all our wet kit, crawled its heavy way, virtually on its knees, to the station and sank into its carriage to be borne to Paris. We were joined in our six-berth sleeper by one unfortunate stranger who, rather sensibly, left us for pastures new quite early on in the night.

Due to the commitments of David's work when he was at the Admiralty, it was almost always I who set off before him, with the children, on far-flung holidays. I towed the caravan all the way to Scotland, where he joined us later and returned home before us, travelling in first class comfort by train.

We crossed the Pentland Firth and returned to our Orkney haunts and friends. Mac Stewart welcomed us back to Hoy Lodge in the north of the island, his cold and somewhat bachelor-uncomfortable house just across the water from Stromness. The long-abandoned and remote hamlet of Rackwick Bay, dwarfed by its huge sea-cliffs and called 'Orkney's last enchantment' by the local poet George McKay Brown, is dotted with a few small ruined houses and almost overlooked by the Old Man of Hoy. Here Nick and Charlotte, now teenagers, had played as very small children, but it was new to Simon, who had been born later in Malta. Mac and David stood, shoeless, on the deserted beach with their trouser legs turned up, like a couple of 1930s gents enjoying a day out at Brighton.

Simon had energetically collected, by hook and probably crook, enough vouchers from his and his prep school friends' copies of the *Eagle* comic, to enable him to make several free day-visits to Butlin's Holiday Camps. He kindly included his siblings and mother as well. On our temporarily fatherless journey home from Scotland, we pulled into the Skegness Butlin's, flourished Simon's vouchers and three of the party had a stupendous day. The fourth enjoyed sitting about and reading. The Bognor Butlin's was also graced with our presence.

19

HMS Mercury

Naval Officers who are Communicators, also referred to as Signal Officers, have a high regard for their division of the Navy and are alleged by others to have a pretty high regard for themselves. Signal Officers naturally refute this view as being completely false. HMS *Mercury*, the Signal School, was a shore establishment, and was situated in Leydene House, between East Meon and Hambledon in Hampshire. Navigating Officers, sometimes termed Wreckers, were, for a time, established in Southwick House, near Portsmouth, as HMS *Dryad*. Sporadic invitations to dinner were exchanged. Before hosting one such occasion, *Dryad* evidently viewed it with some apprehension. This is the first verse of a longer poem, author unknown, quoted in his book *Signal!* by a one-time Captain of the Signal School, Barrie Kent.

> *Start fattening the calves and decanting the wine;*
> *The Lords of the Ether are coming to dine.*
> *The pillars of fashion are donning their best*
> *To visit the Wreckers who dwell Sou'-Sou'-West.*

To be appointed Captain of *Mercury* was regarded as the peak of a Signal Officer's career. We arrived just before

Christmas, 1963, for David to assume this post. We were to attend the Carol Concert as our first appearance at Leydene House. The children were polished up and threatened with 'dire consequences' should any misdemeanours occur. Five huge leather armchairs in the front row awaited us. Simon almost disappeared into his, legs completely straight out in front. Charlotte managed to get her feet over the edge, but rising out of these chairs to sing the occasional carol standing was, even for adults, quite a struggle. Everyone behaved well so there were no dire consequences.

There was no Captain's house at Leydene. (Signal Officers who entertained hopes of becoming *Mercury*'s Captain in the future and who were sufficiently well-endowed to do so bought suitable houses in the vicinity. We fell into neither of these categories.) We rented The Priory, an erstwhile religious establishment, in the nearby village of Chalton. This became our 'stately home' period, complete with an alleged friendly ghost in the kitchen. Only Woolley, the dog, appeared to notice the 'presence' and backed out barking fiercely with hackles bristling.

David came home from *Mercury* one evening to find the house empty, the kitchen sink splodged with a great deal of blood and bloody drying-up cloths adorning the floor. Since he had no way of finding out what these signs presaged, but was reassured by the fact that no bodies littered the scene, he quietly continued with his crossword and awaited developments.

Was he the least bit anxious, with imagined scenes of carnage disturbing his concentration? Had we all been kidnapped after putting up a particularly gory but brave fight? He certainly appeared relieved when, some time later, I arrived back from the local surgery with Charlotte, and a stitched-up Simon no longer leaking blood. He and Charlotte had been watching children's television and when a natural break came with an advertisement, he had dashed into the kitchen for a drink. With only socks on his feet he had slid involuntarily across the floor, hitting the sink very quickly and extremely violently and cutting his chin wide open.

With no time to leave a message (and mobile phones not having been invented) I had scooped them both into the car, leaving behind a scene reminiscent of a minor massacre. (One wonders if other families have quite so many stitchable wounds attended to. This one was by no means the last.) David said to Charlotte later, when the drama had subsided, that he *knew* we'd be all right "with Mummy in charge".

Simon attended a nearby happy little village school where he idled enjoyably with his fellow pupils, managing to learn to read by the age of six. The school was perfectly contented, then, to have outdoor lavatories situated at the far end of the playground. This did no-one any harm even when it rained though Health and Safety would nowadays disapprove.

He went to Horris Hill when he was nearly eight. (This is a decision that I would never take now, being convinced that children need to be with their parents and their mother in particular, until they are at least twelve or thirteen. 'I am just OK,' he wrote home, heartrendingly. But we had little choice, being on the move roughly every two years.)

Charlotte went to a weekly boarding school in Winchester, where she spent Mondays to Fridays longing for the weekends and Saturdays and Sundays dreading Monday. When eventually she went to my old school, St Mary's, Calne, as a full-time boarder, she was much more settled, even if we, her parents, were abroad.

The owner of Chalton Priory had wanted us to take the house for three years, his work having been relocated to Yorkshire for that time. Naval appointments are generally for two years so we were reluctant to tie ourselves up for so long. Eventually he agreed to the two years. Ironically, in the event,

David's time at *Mercury* was extended by six months and the owner's time in Yorkshire reduced by a year, so he wanted it back before we were ready to leave.

He came to visit us as we were reluctantly packing up to move to a Married Quarter for the remaining time. "Have you enjoyed living here?" he enquired of seven-year-old Simon.

"Yes, thank you, but a horrid man is coming to take it away," was the innocent, embarrassing, but uncompromising reply.

20

Chatham Again

The town of Chatham is not a particularly beautiful place but the Navy has had an important base there and thereabouts on the river Medway since, in 1547, an annual rent of thirteen shillings and fourpence was paid for a storehouse at Gillingham.

We returned in 1966, four years after the end of our last appointment there, when David became the Captain of the Dockyard. Our five-storey house was the first one in a terrace of beautiful eighteenth century buildings. The kitchen was in the cellar with a rope-operated lift to the dining room above. Over that was the double drawing room overlooking the Admiral's house with a view of the river beyond. The large bedrooms occupied the top two floors. The house came equipped with a couple of not altogether satisfactory naval staff – a cook and a general dogsbody – whose marital and personal problems occupied at least some of my time.

Woolley, an independently-minded dog, took himself for walks round the Dockyard and was well-known by the ship-builders and other Dockyard 'maties'. He would be greeted with shouts of "Hullo, Woolley," from complete strangers when we walked with him. At one time he went missing. Notices were put up. 'Woolley is lost. Have you seen him?'

One of life's mysteries was that he was eventually found in one of the elegant houses in the terrace which happened to be empty of tenants at the time.

Nick was now at Winchester. Our translations round the world at roughly two-year intervals made boarding for the children an educational necessity but it was a heart-tearing effort to see them off each term. When Charlotte and Simon eventually boarded too, I drove home after leaving them at their new schools, half-blinded by tears.

My father-in-law's eldest half-brother, Sir Arthur Morgan (he was given the K for being the President of the Law Society but was known throughout the family as Uncle Bip, for reasons long forgotten) had been a founder pupil at Horris Hill, at the turn of the nineteenth century. He was followed later by Vaughan, and, in the early Thirties, by David. Myth, had it that anyone who had, as a boy, endured the rigours of HH, could manage the horrors of the trenches of the First World War with equanimity. It was, by now, a somewhat more gentle institution. Even so, Simon's two front teeth were knocked out early on by some accident and were replaced by shiny gold ones. Later, in Singapore, this raised his standing considerably among the Chinese.

We acquired a small caravan which we used for holidays and in which we visited the children at school. In the winter terms it was pretty chilly, the water-tap producing crushed ice in the mornings and the windows opaque with beautiful frost patterns.

Pupils then had few of the 'leave-outs' that they enjoy nowadays, seemingly every other weekend. Even so, when we were in Singapore, we had to rely on the children's Aunt Prue (Le Fanu) to field them from their schools at the beginning and end of terms and, occasionally, to arrange for the great excitement of being driven to Heathrow by Michael's official driver. "Come on, Mr Spillane, do a ton up the M4," they urged him. (I'm not saying if he ever did.)

Skiing now entered our lives. Admiral Sir John Parker, David's immediate superior in Chatham and a close friend, was a great enthusiast. Simon broke both legs – one each on two separate occasions – early on in his skiing career. My two sisters and I, together with our numerous progeny – Diana's five, Camilla's four and my three – plus Camilla's husband, Michael, as the only adult male – travelled *en masse* to Andermatt by train. At least, all of us did except Charlotte and me. She broke up from school later than the rest so we flew out a day or so after to join the others.

On the way out, we learned, they had all alighted to stretch their legs at Basle and were piling back in again when the whistle blew and the train began to move off. Several were still on the platform. With great presence of mind, Tim, Diana's eldest, pulled the communication cord. The train jolted to a stop. It appeared that nothing even approaching the heinousness of this act had ever before occurred on the Swiss railway system. Officials were not amused. Names were taken, addresses noted, deep offence expressed. Nothing more was ever heard of the affair.

We had a jolly holiday till Simon broke a leg and was carted off to hospital down the valley. My skiing week was truncated yet again as he and I flew home early with his leg in plaster. He was admitted to a men's ward in the Westminster Hospital since all the children's beds were full. The newspaper man came round in the morning. "D'you want a paper, Sonny?" he asked kindly.

"Yes, please, I'll have *The Times*," was the reply of the eight-year-old, while the surrounding readers of the Sun and Express giggled behind their papers.

The second fracture occurred when he went skiing with his prep school. On the evening of the first day of their trip to France I was phoned by the master in charge of the party.

In a slow and gloomy voice he announced, "I'm very sorry to tell you, Mrs Morgan, that Simon has had an accident." Instantly, in my imagination, I had him lost over a precipice, brain-damaged, maimed for life in some frightful way or even dead.

"He's broken his leg," went on the voice. What a relief! I thought of saying "Is that all?" but felt it sounded somewhat casual. This might have put some people permanently off the sport. He continues to ski, however, in the most elegant way (as they all do) whenever he gets the chance.

21

From Sink to Mink

From Chatham we crossed the world to Singapore leaving all three children at school. It was May 1968. Nick was at Winchester College, Charlotte at my old school, St Mary's, and Simon at HH. David became the romantic-sounding Captain of the Fleet, first among equals of the 'Captains' Club', which consisted of about five other officers.

Alighting from the RAF plane in Changi airport in Singapore was like entering an oven warm enough to cook meringues. A wave of heat rose from the tarmac and hit one straight between the eyes. Tiredness, jet-lag, the wrench of being so far away from the children, the mass of strangers with their forgettable names, all combined to make the first few days miserable. It was early spring and the whole summer term in England, not to mention eight thousand miles, stretched between us and the children's holidays. They would fly out as unaccompanied minors, labelled like luggage, twice a year.

At last, amongst a throng of other parents, we met them at Changi. The two boys could be seen in the crowd of children pouring off the plane.

"Where is Charlotte?" we enquired of them anxiously.

"Oh, they nearly took her off the plane when we stopped

in Bangkok", said Nick. "She was sick the whole way and they thought she was too ill to go on. In the end they allowed her back on and they're just cleaning her up. Look, there she is."

A pale wraith of a girl tottered down the plane's steps, supported by a stewardess, and fell into our arms. It was the start of a lifetime's air-sickness.

The children were flown out for only two of the three annual school holidays. I went home for the Easter break, took the children skiing with my sisters and their young, coped with Simon's broken leg and got them all back to school. On my return flight to Singapore at the end of the holidays (courtesy of the RAF) some extremely minor adjustment to the aircraft necessitated an overnight stay on the island of Gan in the Indian Ocean. I like to think that, though probably only an ash-tray had fallen off, the military population of the island (being exclusively male) had negotiated some arrangement with the RAF, such that the entire planeload of mostly female passengers was required to stay for twenty-four hours. The sun went down leaving an after-glow of considerable beauty and an instant Summer Ball was organised under the stars and the palm trees, with the gentle sound of the Indian Ocean lapping the beach. Our husbands had to put up with our absence and meet us in Changi a day later.

Our house was the only modern one in the naval base of HMS *Terror*. Its predecessor on the site had been bombed during some fracas or other. It had one air-conditioned bedroom and three hot ones. Simon often slept on the balcony under a mosquito net. He was rearing four tiny frogs, raised from tadpoles. Regardless of gender they were called Charles, Philip, Arthur and George after the Prince of Wales. Their exercise consisted of climbing up the inside of the mosquito net while Simon lolled on his bed urging them on. Eventually they were accidentally washed down a monsoon drain, hunted for in great distress by Simon but never seen again.

The wife of the Commander-in-Chief, Far East, was a very diffident, shy and reserved woman. Even after years of marriage to a very senior officer, the social side of this role was clearly agony for her. During one particular dinner party, at the end of the meal the hostess silently 'collected the eyes' of the ladies, who then rose from the dining table like a cloud of multi-coloured butterflies, to flutter gracefully to the drawing room, leaving the gentlemen to their port and masculine chat. Once dotted about with the coffee, the conversation languished.

We did our nervous best to prop it upright but it kept falling silently prostrate and had to be given the kiss of a frail sort of life, such observations as to how lovely the flowers were looking standing in for anything more intelligent or profound. The weather, such a safe cliché subject when all else fails, at least in a temperate and changeable climate, is no good in the tropics.

"Did you enjoy your recent visit to Hong Kong?" someone ventured to enquire of our hostess.

"Yes, thank you, it was very pleasant. Would you like some more coffee?"

Anything for a slight diversion. "Thank you so much, yes, I would." The bell was rung, the head steward summoned, fresh coffee brought, cups filled. "Sugar, Madam?" Dresses were rearranged, hair patted, small talk revived.

I longed to say something outrageous such as – "What is your view of original sin, Lady X?" The shock wave might have livened-up proceedings considerably or else have stopped, entirely, all further attempts at conversation. It would certainly have saved me, at least, from all future invitations. It was probably concern for our husbands' careers that was so brain-disabling.

Eventually, after what felt like a very long wait, the men,

most of whom spent the best part of every day working in each other's company, emerged from their enjoyable male enclave and joined the ladies. There was an almost audible tremor of relief and, as soon as politely possible, we expressed our thanks for a delightful evening, escaped to our cars and waiting drivers and went home.

The Navy had a wise saying, 'Sink to Mink and back to Sink'. This meant that from time to time an appointment took a family from their own home or Married Quarter – Sink – and transformed it to Mink in the form of high quality accommodation (and in places like Singapore) house-servants, a gardener or two, a chap to squirt the monsoon drains with anti-mosquito stuff and a driver with an official car. At the end of the appointment, the family returned to Sink – or, in other words, normal life. Singapore was our Mink period. After a time, I decided to enjoy it, artificiality and all.

Tennis in the cool early mornings, learning to water-ski, boat picnics, pretending to play golf, painting classes, shopping at CK Tang's in Orchard Road and far too much of a social life all filled the time. It was fairly normal to attend two cocktail parties and a dinner party on the same evening. At weekends there were picnics up the east coast of Malaysia, reached through jungle and plantations of oil palms and bananas and by crossing rivers on rickety ferries. Sometimes a night or two would be spent in the Rest House in Mersing, where the dusk was deafening with the shouts of cicadas. The seemingly unending racket of the aptly-named brain-fever bird also drilled its way into one's skull.

There was an island off Mersing where friends of ours often camped. We called it Arthur's Isle. Arthur, though one of David's fellow Captains, was a hen-pecked husband continually at the beck, and even more the call, of his large and powerful wife. The ringing cry of "*Arthur*" was the vocal accompaniment of many an outing we shared with them.

The Rev. William Lewis Rosedale né Rosenthal,
my great grandfather.

Caroline Anne Rosedale née Gough,
my great grandmother.

Caroline's mother, Katharine Gough
née Tunnicliffe.

The Rev. Richard Edward Pell Edmonds,
father of Caroline Bertha Jagger,
my maternal grandmother.

Caroline Bertha Jagger née Edmonds,
my maternal grandmother.

Frances Edmonds née Arnold,
Richard's wife, known as Fanny.

Canon James Edwin Jagger,
my maternal grandfather.

'Us', as my mother called this photo of
herself, aged seventeen, and her parents.

Marjorie Bertha Rosedale née Jagger,
my mother, known as Peggy.

William Oriel Pelly Rosedale,
my father, known as Rio.

Honyel Gough Rosedale, Rio's father.

Ada Rosedale née Pelly, Rio's mother.

Sir John Henry Pelly 1852, 1st Baronet,
Rio's great grandfather.

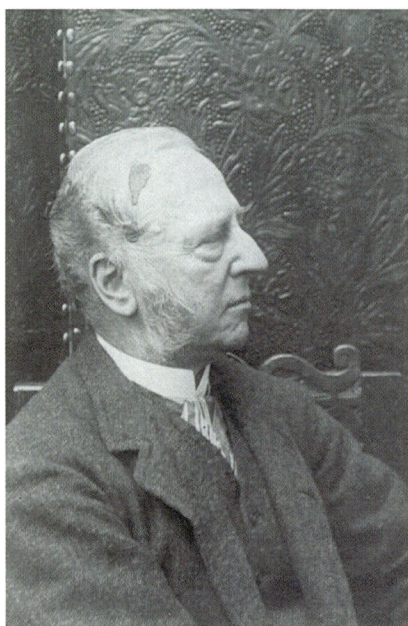
Percy Leonard Pelly,
Rio's grandfather.

L to R Diana, Camilla and Stephanie Rosedale c1931.

James Oriel Bernard Rosedale, known as Barney, aged three, 1939.

Young Rosedales 1980. Rupert, Lawrence, Ben and Kath with their parents, Barney and Rachel née Cripps.

King's Prizegiving 1950.

David's and my wedding, August 1950.

L to R Syb, Vaughan, Arthur, Ed,
Richard and Kit Morgan 1895. (Mary not yet born.)

Elizabeth Morgan,
David's sister, known as Libby.

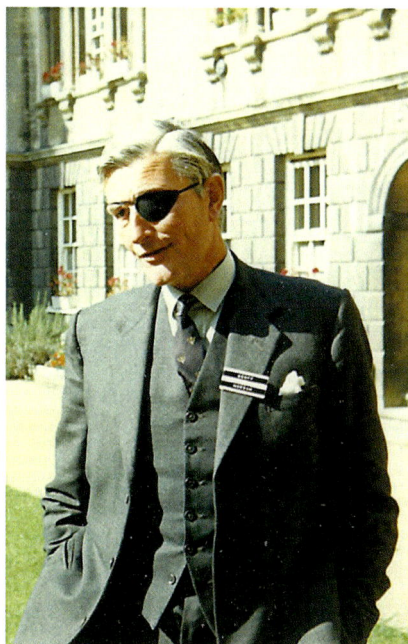

Geoffrey Morgan,
David's first cousin.

The Rosedale Siblings 1987.

David Morgan, 1978.

Stephanie Morgan, 2005.

Barney Rosedale, my brother.

Charlotte Maizels, my daughter.

Charlotte with James, Lucy and Tom Maizels.

Simon Morgan, my younger son.

Surgeon Captain Nicholas Morgan RN
and BA Captain Simon Morgan
with their proud mother.

Caroline Morgan, my eldest grandchild.

Caroline and her brother, Chris Morgan.

Anna and Jack Morgan, Simon and Sally's twins.

Rupert Rosedale,
Barney and Rachel's eldest son.

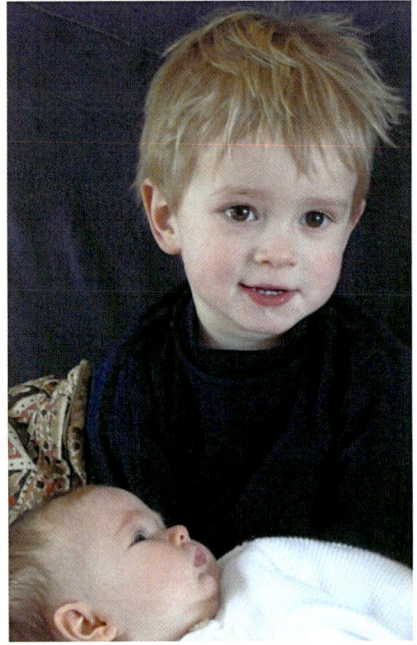

Ted and Svea Rosedale,
Rupert and Ulrika's children.

Our father, Rio, on his 80th birthday
with our gift to him – a picture of
'The Three Graces.'

With our mother.

Occasionally we could escape the humid heat of Singapore Island and drive up to the cool Highlands in central Malaysia. Here, at Fraser's Hill, one or two of the Rest Houses were maintained for the relaxation of the British Forces and were a throw-back to Edwardian times. The lavatory seats were purest mahogany with polished brass fittings, afternoon tea was served with fine bone china, sandwiches and cakes, fires were lit in the chilly evenings and hot water bottles tenderly placed in beds. We played golf in a desultory way but mostly we relaxed.

Nick went on an expedition up country with local people during one summer holiday, riding the rivers of Malaysia through virgin jungle and eating almost nothing but curry. We practically never had curry for lunch in our house but, on the day he unexpectedly returned home at lunch-time from this rather trying journey, we had been persuaded by the cook to try some. Nick's look of disbelief as he encountered yet another meal of his far-from-favourite food was memorable.

It felt strange to be water-skiing in the morning of Christmas Day but in the evening we joined the Admiral Superintendent's family for Christmas dinner, facing turkey and pudding under the circling fan. The hot and humid air moved sluggishly about. As the night proceeded, this fan became the target for streamers and other missiles until its load of coloured paper caused it, with a final creak, to cease circling. A man was sent for and it was time to go home to bed.

Another naval wife Marian and I joined a group arranged by the local Automobile Association to visit Cambodia. This was some time before Pol Pot and the Vietnam War. After strolling along Phnom Penh's bustling streets with throngs of colourful people bargaining for goods and exotic foods and flowers, we flew on, over the huge lake of Tonlé Sap, to Siem Reap.

Here we could enjoy (in peaceful ignorance of the

horrors of the Khmer Rouge regime yet to come) the glories of twelfth century Angkor Wat, the largest religious temple in the world. Its five tall towers were reflected in its moat, intricate carvings adorned its walls and saffron-robed monks strolled along its cloisters. A great many other temples are dotted about in the region, many rescued from the worst of the encroaching jungle but some still with great trees growing through their walls.

Marian's snoring was gentle. It was my ear-splitting scream ("Loud enough to wake the dead," she murmured sleepily), when a cockroach sauntered over my face in the night, that woke her up. I despatched it but others lurked, one of them in her wash-bag. Tourism was in its infancy in Cambodia and the standard of some hotels allowed the insects the free run of bedrooms.

Back in Phnom Penh, a beautiful city floating on the banks of the Mekong and other rivers, a visit to the Royal Museum was enlivened by the sight of a splendid bowler hat, adorned with several large diamonds including one of fifty carats. (Not altogether suitable, I felt, for a London City gent or even a Cambodian one.)

Another outing was to Japan. The Commander-in-Chief flew officially to visit Tokyo and invited people to fill up his plane for a small consideration. A friend and I headed the queue. A three-day coach tour seemed the best way of seeing something of the country. It was autumn and the trees were everywhere gloriously coloured as we drove past minutely manicured fields – every blade of rice up to its proper work – to Kyoto. Here were gardens filled with flowers and flawlessly raked sand, beautiful lakes, temples, monasteries, shrines and the constant background of snow-topped Mount Fuji.

At meals in hotels, we sat on the floor with our feet in a square hole under the table and ate the sort of food described by Flanders and Swann as 'aubergine and carnation petals'.

There was a frisson of alarm on my part when we were threatened with communal nude bathing but this turned out to be 'The Joke', practised on female foreigners for the pleasure of the locals.

We whizzed back to Tokyo in the bullet train in what seemed like a matter of seconds, to the high-rise glass buildings, the flashy shops and the garish lights, the excitement and the traffic, the noise and the crowds of almost any capital city. We also tried a smattering of a Japanese play but were forced to retreat in the face of our complete inability to make head or tail of the story.

22

Walking in the Foothills

From Singapore I thumbed a lift in the eight-seater Army plane of a Brigadier who was going to inspect the Ghurkas in Nepal. Barney was working there and I had yet to meet Rachel, his recently acquired wife. Due to a certain amount of incompetence on my part and the fact that I had only just returned from a trip to Hong Kong, I had failed to get a visa before we set off. The Army Major, who met us when we paused in Calcutta and to whom I confessed my visa-less state, was aghast.

"How did you expect to go on to Nepal without one?" he enquired testily, scorn for females of all kinds, especially those without visas, marring his excellent features.

Trepidation caused my knees to knock as I envisaged the awful ignominy of being put on the next plane back to Singapore.

"I thought I had read that it is possible to get one at the Nepalese Embassy here," I quavered.

"Not," he said, even more testily, "at 5.00 pm when the Embassy closes at midday."

I brought the full battery of feminine charm, such as it was, to bear, throwing myself on his mercy with batted eyelashes and pleas for help. Was it the result of this or his dreadful fear of having me left on his hands? To my relief, he managed to rouse some unfortunate Nepalese Consul General from his relaxing bath and coerce him into putting his signature to the lovely purple hieroglyphics stamped in my passport.

We landed in Biratnager in south-east Nepal on a grass runway from which the cattle and goats had been induced by a small boy to depart. Barney and Rachel emerged from a cloud of dust and a white Land Rover. We simply drove away from the hut which served as the air-terminal and no-one asked to see my passport. I had been wasting my charm on the irate Major, and the Consul General had kindly allowed his bath water to get cold for nothing.

Requested useful articles like biros, sticky tape and razor blades and delicious things like cheese, Marmite and booze, were unpacked to much appreciation. Barney showed me, with a becoming modesty masking his immense pride, the various improvements the Britain-Nepal Medical Trust team had managed to achieve on the proverbial shoestring, in a country where TB is practically endemic. On Market and Fair days, the team would set up its stall and induce passers-by to roll up and have their BCG vaccinations. In this way they hoped to catch young people who might otherwise slip through the net and remain vulnerable.

Barney announced that we were all going off for a trek in the foothills for a few days. With the minimum of preparation, it seemed to me, we drove thirty miles to where the road ended and the hills began and started walking. Several porters appeared and set off with us, each carrying sixty-pound loads in conical baskets, or *dokas*, suspended from their foreheads with wide webbing. These contained medical stores and drugs to be dotted about in various hill villages so that patients could be treated close to home.

It was hot and the walk mostly uphill. An icy cold stream

provided a brief cooling off. When I caught up with the rest of them at the first tea-house, I was painfully aware that the kind of life I led in Singapore wasn't at all a good preparation for walking about in the foothills of the Himalayas. By what felt like lunch-time, there was no sign of lunch.

"I fancy a smoked salmon sandwich," I remarked without hope. "Ha ha!" they said politely and pressed me to have another mug of tea and a piece of sugar cane. I discovered very quickly that if tea is all you get, all day, sugar in it is absolutely necessary and I even began to like it.

The rest of the journey was long enough for my leg muscles to reach an exquisite state of real agony, but not quite long enough for them to recover. The stony and precipitous path was the main road into the hills, with porters and other people coming and going, mostly heavily laden. The first night was spent at a little *bati* or inn. A meal, into which a bit of old goat had crept, tasted in my lunchless state, completely delicious. Yawning, we climbed the ladder to the flat roof made of dried mud, lay in our sleeping bags under the stars in a row on the ground and fell asleep instantly.

It was only later, in the dark, surrounded by the sound of gentle snoring, that I woke and made three discoveries. The first was that excruciating stiffness had set in from the waist down and the second that the human form is the wrong shape for sleeping on dried mud floors. The third was that the sanitary arrangements being non-existent, the process of having a pee, involving getting out of the sleeping bag, stepping over six recumbent sleepers and the dog, not falling off the roof, descending the ladder and finding a convenient patch of someone's back yard, all by moonlight, was too complicated. The rest of the night was patchy.

In the coolness of the early day, we climbed up from the river. The lovely little town of Dhankuta, perched high on a ridge, boasted a cobbled street, balconied houses with wooden carvings, small delightful children, blazing flowers and a mountain backdrop. To improve matters still further, lunch appeared to be part of the programme.

In the next early dawn, the sun's light slanted sideways onto the eastern flanks of the formidable mountains, turning their snow pink and gold, and their sunless sides into enormous dark shadowy shapes. Their powerful vastness was fifty miles away, separated from us only by misty foothills. The panorama was unforgettable.

All would have been well had Rachel and I, walking back alone, not bought and eaten the sourest and most acidic grapefruit I had ever encountered. Barney and the dog had marathoned on, leaving us to return in as leisurely a way as the switchbacking hills allowed. We dangled our feet in an icy river and, with many a grimace, devoured the refreshing but nearly death-dealing fruit. An hour later, plodding grimly on, I was fighting off both nausea and a grave internal turmoil. We stumbled alongside a dried-up river bed and came suddenly upon an astonishing sight.

The Brigadier and his wife, in whose Army plane to Nepal we had all flown from Singapore and whom I had known there, were ensconced in comfortable chairs in true British Raj fashion, enjoying glasses of something alcoholic. We looked about us at the perfectly pitched tents, the three porters neatly stacking stores and the cook preparing supper over an efficient fire.

"May I enquire," said the Brigadier, rising from his portable chair and raising his hat, "what you two ladies think you are doing, walking alone in the hills without so much as a single porter?"

"And," he went on, glancing at me, "one of you looks fit to die." He sent a porter for the medicine chest who staggered back with it.

Fortunately it was found to contain antidotes for all

known ills. We pondered which of the many remedies to apply and finally chose some large and powerful looking tablets – sixteen to be taken at once and four every four hours. After this exacting task, a little whiskey was prescribed all round. The cure began.

The Brigadier was politely horrified to find two *Memsahibs* travelling alone, though what potential fate he had in mind for us was not disclosed. He had only known me as the wife of a comparatively senior naval officer in the social whirl of Singapore, and could hardly reconcile this knowledge with the somewhat different version wilting before him. I was glad that he was not present later when Rachel and I dossed down at the next *bati* in the horizontal company of a great many porters, to the accompaniment of the noises of sleeping humanity and other fauna.

Though my personal inner tumult was subsiding slightly, it was well worth not sleeping too well that night. An enormous and beautiful full moon rose from behind the hill and passed lustrously overhead, illuminating the little huddle of buildings, the tethered animals, the river bed and my path to the nearest bushes. More than five hundred lunar months later, a gleaming Harvest moon, hanging over the South Downs, brings back this radiant memory.

The women we encountered on the path back, elegant in their long skirts, giggled and stared at our short cotton dresses and stout boots. Evidently, far too much leg was being shown for polite society as we crawled from patch to patch of shade in the increasing heat. After a teeth-gritting uphill grind, going down was merely a change of pain. My legs were forced to hold out till the plains and 'home' were reached. We fell asleep for hours and hours, had a shower and slept again.

The Army plane had long since returned to Singapore and the civil one that took me back to Calcutta gave the impression of being held together with string and sticking plaster. The hotel there, with its hot water, clean sheets and perfectly served food, was in shattering contrast to the beggar-ridden, garbage-filled streets. From its cool windows people could be seen sleeping on doorsteps. Wealthy Singapore was a world away.

The British Colonial and naval world seemed to be closing down as we moved around the globe. Scapa Flow was mothballed soon after we left there, Malta was finished as an important naval base as we left, Chatham was closed later, HMS *Mercury* eventually moved to Fareham, and Singapore was abandoned to much tear-jerking playing of *The Last Post* and lowering of flags. From there we flew home with a short pause in Cyprus, from which we departed, stuffed into the back of the Air Force plane along with a great many cauliflowers and oranges. The RAF transport authorities had taken the name 'Captain Morgan' as that of an Army officer and therefore of a much lower rank. They were visibly surprised when 'Captain Morgan' was met with a car and driver and, divesting himself of vegetables and fruit, was escorted off the plane first. It would never have occurred to David to 'pull rank' and complain.

23

A Home at Last

We had moved house fourteen times in twenty years, gathering many an acquaintance and several close friends. From the summer of 1950, two years had been spent in London in two different flats, another two-and-a-half years in Swanmore, Hampshire, where Charlotte was added to the family, and a further year-and-a-half in Scapa Flow in Orkney. After that it was Malta, (autumn '56 to May '59) where Simon joined us, followed by Chatham for two years, then, horribly, New Malden for one year and Bath, enjoyably, for another. The shore establishment of HMS *Mercury* came next, from Christmas '63 to May '66, (changing for the last six months, from Stately Home to Married Quarter), and then Chatham again for two years. From there we flew to Singapore in '68, back to Pulborough in 1970 and the search for a home.

We had no house in England so we perched in my parents' cottage in Pulborough, adjusting ourselves slowly to normal life. The summer was spent trying to find a house that we liked and the difficulties of acquiring a mortgage were as tiresome in 1970 as they are now (2009 onwards). I had a permanent hovering headache. We tramped round the country. Too big, too small, not in the right place, just didn't like it, already sold, too expensive, too decrepit, not enough

garden, too much garden – the perfect house evaded us...
And then my mother saw an advertisement in a Sunday paper
for Noddswood, a five bedroom house (well, five if you count
the two bedrooms squashed into the roof under the eaves) on
the outskirts of South Harting, on the borders of West Sussex
and Hampshire. We had found, at last, what we wanted.

"What about fifteen thousand pounds? Would the
owners accept that?" David asked the estate agent tentatively.
He smirked.

"I'm afraid not, sir. We already have an offer of that."
He studied his finger nails and waited.

"Give them another thou, Dad," said Nick generously.
(Nowadays, this would be like suggesting a doubling of the
price.) We gulped. Bravely, knees shaking, we made the offer.

"*Sixteen thousand pounds!*" exclaimed Prue when she
heard of this outrageous sum. "No Morgan can afford that."
(Only a few years later, in a climate of wild house-price
inflation, she eventually came to live in Harting, and was
forced to pay more than twice this amount for Park Cottage.)

"I'll ask the owners to consider your proposal," the
estate agent remarked in a bored fashion, just as if this was
not the most crucial and expensive step in our lives. (Twenty-
three years later, I sold it for about two hundred and thirty
thousand pounds and it is probably worth a million now that
the present owners have improved it yet again.)

We moved in on 1st July 1970. Charlotte picked up
some gravel from the drive and held it in her hand. "To
think we actually own even these stones," she exclaimed in
an incredulous voice, the voice of a pillar-to-post child of
nomadically moving parents. We had tried to make wherever
we were stationed into 'home', but for all of us, this was a
truly significant moment – a delayed planting of roots and a
new sense of permanence.

The house had once been two farm-workers' cottages,

built a hundred years earlier and now knocked into one and enlarged, with a view up to the South Downs across fields and woods and a long drive back to the road. Everyone could now make as much noise as they liked, there being no neighbours to disturb.

Woolley, the Peke, had been left with friends on our departure to Singapore. Loved and fed till he was barrel-shaped, the friends contemplated his return to us with barely concealed tears. It was kindest to leave him. A bracken-coloured spaniel now joined the family – so we called him Bracken.

Simon raised yet another litter of tadpoles, leaving them to me for safe keeping when he went back to school. As they grew into tiny frogs they ate greenfly. I collected these by brushing them off the roses. I was the only person in the whole of the South of England who *ran out* of greenfly. I resorted to dog food on which the froglets became fat and lazy and probably resented being released into a local pond where they had to fend for themselves.

"Why don't you come back to nursing?" enquired the matron of the Petersfield Cottage Hospital wielding an efficient needle as she stitched up a saw-inflicted wound on Nick's hand. We had mentioned that he was a medical student at the London Hospital and that I had, what seemed a lifetime ago, been a qualified nurse.

Four months' part-time work at this small hospital proved a useful re-introduction to the now much-moved-on world of medicine. Then, in the autumn of 1973, Camilla and I set off on a Major Adventure. This saga, of an eleven-week overland journey from Victoria Station to Kathmandu, will appear, together with other travellers' tales, in a separate volume.

24

Macmillan Years

The King Edward VII Hospital near Midhurst, built in the early twentieth century with money extracted by the monarch from his rich friends and relations, was originally a sanatorium. TB was then rife and people spent years there, lying on the wide balconies, enjoying the views to the South Downs and trying to recover.

"I'm going to write a book and learn Spanish," said one patient optimistically, contemplating the months ahead. But, "There's never enough time or energy," she complained later, when asked how the book was getting on.

Eventually, with TB all but (temporarily) conquered, the place became a private general hospital. On my return from the dramas of the overland expedition, I worked there as a slightly rusty Staff Nurse for three days a week. A couple of years later, in 1976, four beds in a medical ward were set aside for a Continuing Care Unit. These catered for patients with cancer from which they were unlikely to recover but whose quality of life could be much improved by symptom-control and other support. Many went home, to enjoy more comfortably what was left of life. I added a fourth working day and visited these patients at home. The Hospice movement was being resurrected from the Middle Ages and it was the beginning of Macmillan Cancer Relief as the charity was then called. It was good to be in at the start of what was to become, nationally and even internationally, a much valued service.

I was the first Home Care Sister, and over the next few years five more joined me. A wing of the hospital was taken over for a twelve-bed unit. My colleagues and I spread ourselves over our 'patches' in a twenty mile radius of the hospital. We carried bleepers which, when they went off, meant we had to ring the hospital to find out why. In the days before mobile phones, I knew the whereabouts of almost every phone box in West Sussex. We supported patients in their own homes and assessed the efficacy of the symptom-relief or the equipment needed. Occasionally we suggested a short stay in the unit to give a family respite or for more thorough assessment and treatment. We co-operated with the district nurses and delicately inducted some of the few rather less enlightened local GPs in the art of adequate pain relief.

I developed a diplomatic phrase for use in their surgeries. "I wonder if you would consider," I would ask tactfully, "writing up some diamorphine for Mrs X," or "allowing Mr Y to increase the dose of his?"

"They'll become addicted to it," they sometimes objected.

Would terminally ill patients have time to do so? Did it matter if, very occasionally, one or two did? This practically never happened and, even if it did, the elimination of pain was surely more important for improving the quality of what remained of life. We reckoned that, since people only die once, it was a good idea to do it as comfortably and peacefully as possible, and preferably at home, both for their sakes and their families'.

It was a rewarding area of work. The feeling of making a difference to a sad and troubled patient and family by offering symptom-control and support of all kinds was deeply satisfying. On one occasion, I made a routine visit to a patient and found, unexpectedly but obviously, that she was dying. Her adult children gathered and talked round her bed, coffee and food were made and laughter and tears came and went. I had known them all for some time and was welcomed as a temporary part of the family. The world outside went noisily and, of course, unconcernedly, on its busy way, while an event as natural but momentous as someone's death was taking place.

It was necessary for one's own sake and mostly possible (but not always), to detach oneself emotionally from the pain of a grieving family. It was much more difficult when the patient was young, questioning and justifiably angry at the hand that Nature had dealt him or her. One young man wanted desperately to take up the University place he had been offered. Nottingham University was admirable for the way it welcomed him, made every arrangement for his comfort and, apart from this concern, treated him no differently from his peers. He survived for half a term, justly proud of what he had achieved, as were his anguished parents.

As often as possible we attended the funerals of those of our patients who died. When Macmillan Headquarters told us we should discontinue this, presumably for financial reasons, we took absolutely no notice. We needed this final act for our own sakes as well as for those of the relatives.

We also had a policy of continuing to visit bereaved relatives until they seemed to be beginning to grip their lives again, but though the numbers made it impossible to persist with the visits for long, groups of the widowed met for mutual support and counselling for as long as they found it helpful. However, one particular widow was so special that she became one of my most valued friends.

Elisabeth and Andrew Kinloch, both architects, had married comparatively late and had enjoyed an excellent but relatively short and childless marriage of about fifteen years when he fell ill and came under the care of the Macmillan Service. They were completely clear as to the inevitable outcome of his illness, could talk about it without gloom and gave small parties in his bedroom, where friends laughed and drank, behaving perfectly normally.

"If you are miserable after my death," Andrew said briskly to Elisabeth, "it'll be your own fault. You must get on with your life and live it."

As far as that is possible, she did. She was a painter in her retirement, taking many a course with the Open College of the Arts and living, it has to be said, in an increasingly chaotic house and garden. Every surface – chairs, the floor, window sills, tables and shelves were covered in papers, letters, old envelopes and cards, paintings, plants, books and flowers, and more spilled out of half open drawers. The garden took over control of itself and flourished gloriously, tall with riotous weeds and rampant unpruned roses. She and I saw each other through many of life's various vicissitudes and we met frequently as close friends. We even joined a painting group holiday on the Greek island of Simi and shared a small villa on the hill overlooking the harbour, during – or rather enduring – the noise, the commotion, even the explosions, of the sort of Easter that only Greeks know how to celebrate.

For a long time her memory became gradually but increasingly rickety. After some twenty-five years of a deeply appreciated friendship, I felt really bereaved that she no longer knew who I was and had no recollection of her marriage, her brother or her nephew and nieces. Nor would a visit, which seemed to be enjoyed in a slightly bewildered way – "Who are you and where do you live?" was repeated again and again – be remembered, I knew, for longer than a few seconds after the door had closed behind me. But at least a kind of disinterested serenity seemed to have replaced previous resentment and anxiety.

The Macmillan Service gave me a gold medal when I retired after thirteen years but I had received and learnt far more during this time than it was possible to give. And when David and I were bidden to Buckingham Palace for a garden party (the invitation being due to the medal and not, as had occurred a couple of times before, because of David's naval service) we didn't actually go. There was a train strike on at the time and we were camping in Savernake Forest with much extended family and were all attending courses at the Marlborough College Summer School. I have no doubt that our absence went completely unnoticed by Her Majesty.

Following a series of adventures in various fairly remote corners of the globe, I was invited to become a Women's Institute speaker and the secretaries of local WIs would book me for their meetings. All went well if the projectors functioned adequately – it's a speaker's nightmare when they don't, as happened to me when I was showing slides of one of my Nepal expeditions to the Harting Society. The projector malfunctioned; a fresh one was spirited from somewhere after a lengthy pause and all the slides hastily – too hastily – were packed into the new holders. Many appeared upside down, back to front and in quite a different order from that intended by me.

One WI lured me to a splendid lunch before the meeting, along with the mainly elderly members, and afterwards we all trouped into a darkened hall for the talk. As it proceeded, I glanced at the nodding heads of the clientele and realised that most of them were having a good post-prandial nap. I experienced a strong urge, which I managed to suppress, to tiptoe out and leave them to their slumbers.

Another time I somehow found myself double-booked, for a talk in the afternoon and another the same evening. The first was a great success, in a hall full of articulate and interested people. In this situation, one makes a good job of the occasion, enjoying the atmosphere, the enthusiasm and the support of the audience.

That same evening a small chilly hall held about a dozen extremely old ladies, hats pulled well down over grey hair. Not the slightest sign of interest could be discerned as my talk proceeded. In these circumstances the chances of being an exhilarating speaker are nil. At the end of the meeting the President said, without a break in the sentence, "Thank you very much Mrs Morgan for your interesting talk the jumble sale will be on Thursday."

25

Nicholas

Nick trained at the London Hospital and lived with some fellow medical students in Cricketfield Road in east London, in what can only be described as Deep Litter. He came down to Noddswood in the winter on his small motor bike, Z-shaped from the cold of the journey and had to be thawed out. He joined the Navy as a medical cadet, partly for the small amount of cash this brought to an impecunious student and partly in the combining of medicine and the Navy in the family tradition.

For his 'Elective' – a few months during training, spent at a medical location of the student's selection – Nick chose a Belfast Hospital for its likely variety of trauma experiences. Before he set off, he visited his godmother, Elizabeth Carnegy of Lour, Forfar, in Scotland. The Bishop of St Andrews was a fellow guest.

"I know of a delightful family called Roemmele who live in Limavady, near Londonderry," said the Bishop, invisibly assuming the role of Cupid and firing off arrows, "who would certainly welcome you to stay during any spare time that you may have. I will write and ask them to be in touch with you."

Bids Roemmele had known the Bishop when she was at school in St Andrews. She was now at Coleraine University

147

and was not impressed at the prospect of the visit. "Not another spotty and probably smelly medical student having to be entertained," she grumbled to her surgeon father, Peter, as she prepared supper with her mother, Jess, prior to Nick's arrival.

"I glanced up as he came into the kitchen," she said later, "and nearly dropped the saucepan." It was not long before they were engaged.

David and I paid a visit to meet the prospective co-in-laws. We sailed from Liverpool to Belfast, the weather forecast predicting very rough seas between the two. Being a poor sailor I took the precaution of swallowing some powerful anti-seasickness pills. We crossed the Irish Sea in an un-foretold flat calm and I could hardly stay awake long enough to be greeted by the new relatives.

One of Bids' brothers was vaguely looking for a country cottage. He and his parents, Nick and Bids, David and I all set off for Donegal and joined in the hunt. We came across a forsaken ruin of a small house at the very back of beyond, roofless and surrounded by nothing but hillocks of sparse vegetation, a few thin sheep and drifting mist. Most of us dismissed it immediately from our minds as a possible place of human habitation. However Peter, the great optimist, after one look at this derelict wreck, made his pronouncement. "Nothing wrong with this wee place," he remarked. "Look at the view – you can't get much better than that."

Jess unpacked a picnic. The very best china, inherited from countless careful ancestors, was unwrapped from its layers of tissue paper and laid out on a tablecloth. Delicious home-made cakes and tiny crustless sandwiches were produced. We were immensely impressed by this refinement – so unlike our own rather more casual picnics – but Bids told me later how she had been embarrassed by the elegance as we huddled out of the wind in the lee of the abandoned homestead. (But then people are often embarrassed by their parents' behaviour.)

Nick and Bids were married in Limavady in August 1977. In spite of the Troubles there, which continued for many years, her parents maintained a neutral attitude to the drawn-out conflict and were respected for this by both sides. Bids just managed to complete her probationary teacher-training year, in September 1978, before Caroline, known ever after, for some obscure reason, as 'Pinks' – arrived at a leisurely pace, taking some two days to do so.

She was joined, nearly four years later and rather more swiftly and dramatically, by Christopher. Not only was he hauled into the world by Caesarean section, but his father managed, only just in time for his son's birth, to return across the world from the Falklands.

The Falklands war, though mercifully short, was a constant, relentless and intense presence in our lives. Every moment, it seemed, the gloomy BBC spokesman brought the nation news and pictures of fresh disasters. It was impossible to think of anything else, even though for part of the time David and I and some of the family were trying to enjoy a previously-booked canal holiday.

I was in my bunk on the boat, listening to the early news. "The Argentineans are saying that they have sunk the *Canberra*," I heard. Nick, now an FRCS, had sailed on her from Southampton and we had no way of knowing either if the news was true or, even if it was, whether he was still on the ship. I went ashore to the nearest village and phoned Bids. In recalling this conversation – in which neither of us knew whether the other was aware of the broadcast and, therefore, both of us were unwilling to speak of it – we can now laugh. We couldn't then. It was far too serious as we both, separately, knew.

In fact we learnt much later that the ship had not been

sunk and Nick was ashore anyway, preparing to operate on the wounded in a disused refrigeration-plant with an unexploded bomb in the roof. His and the other surgeons' contributions to the welfare of the wounded, all of whom, if brought alive to the makeshift theatre, left alive, were recorded in a book, *The Red and Green Life Machine* (the colours of the Army and the Royal Marines) written by Surgeon Commander Rick Jolly who was in charge of the place.

Lebanon, in the Middle East, was aflame with one of a series of small but destructive wars and should have occasioned more of my concern. It was, however, low on my list of worries. The small islands in the south Atlantic were the focus of every waking moment. "Did it ever cross your mind," I asked Nick later, "that you might be wounded or worse?"

He looked astonished. "Never," he said. "I was far too busy."

There was a train strike on at the time of Christopher's birth. After inspecting Charlotte's James, who was born in the Paddington Hospital, I caught a sleepless overnight coach to Plymouth to meet his first cousin Christopher, born just twenty-four hours before him. I arrived in the dawn of a gleaming July morning and sat peacefully in the sun in the garden till discovered by an early-tea-making Nick, only just back from the Falklands war.

We watched, on television, the triumphant return of the *Canberra* into Portsmouth harbour on her homecoming from the same war. It was extremely emotional, after all the anxieties of the last weeks, to feel deeply for the families of those who would not be coming back but to be thankful, not only for Nick's safe return and the end of the brief war, but also for the happy arrival of the two babies.

The not-quite-four-year-old Caroline, remembering her bearded father who had set out to war only a few months before, failed momentarily to recognise the clean-shaven Nick on his return. Tentatively she said, "I don't think we've been introduced."

Bids and he lived in Plymouth where she worked as a primary school teacher as the children grew up. In 1997 she was asked to set up and run the nursery and pre-prep for Mount House, a prep school on the outskirts of Tavistock. This was a huge task which she carried out for eight years triumphantly and very successfully in the face of quite a few difficulties and obstructions.

Christopher went to a nursery school where he won a prize for being the best sleeper in Rest Time. He was a natural swimmer almost from birth. People asked his parents anxiously, as they watched him cruising along under water, "Are you sure your baby's not drowning?"

Delightful as a small boy, delightful as an adult, he moved, via Kelly College in Tavistock and spells in both Greece and Antigua with Sunsail, (who had originally hired him to teach wind-surfing) to follow his vocation as an extremely good photographer.

Naval doctors cater medically for the Royal Marines as well as for the Navy. For Nick to be accepted as an equal by the 'Royals', he clearly had to earn his Green Beret, the coveted reward at the end of a long and gruelling course which tests the participants both physically and mentally. During part of it, he and his fellow contestants in 42 Commando were camping in the dead of winter. I heard on the radio that deep snow covered Exmoor. "Nothing and nobody could be alive on the moor," said the reporter gloomily. I rather hoped that there were a few exceptions to this pronouncement.

Nick enjoyed a varied career, very much a part of his greatly-admired Royal Marines for a good deal of it, and visited many far-flung portions of the globe including Tuvalu in the Pacific and, of course, the rather too exciting Falklands.

For the last couple of years, until he retired from the Navy as a Surgeon Captain, he spent almost every weekday in the Ministry of Defence in London (housed by the MOD in increasingly depressing flats) and travelled home at weekends.

Soon after Bids began work on the pre-prep school she and Nick moved some eighteen miles from Plymouth to near Tavistock. They bought Bedford House in the Dartmoor National Park. This required a considerable amount of renovating. The river Walkham formed the southern boundary of the ten acres of garden, fields and steep woods that became their property. Once free from the Navy, Nick and Bids were hard at work with hens, ducks, uninvited free-loading guests in the form of five guinea fowl, vegetable-growing, mowing, dog-walking, managing the woods and much else. Later, pigs joined the menagerie, producing tasty pork and huge numbers of sausages for barbecues at family gatherings.

To own a boat had been one of Nick's ambitions for a long time. Over the years he had become qualified as a yacht master and on his retirement he was at last able to acquire a catamaran. This had been fastidiously built over some six years by an American who then decided, reluctantly, that he was too old to sail in her. Sadly, he advertised it for sale and Nick bought it. She was lying in a marina in Florida. In February 2010, I was invited by Nick and Bids to come aboard for a sailing holiday in the 'Sunshine State'.

Accepting this kind invitation, but not being any sort of a sailor, I announced to Nick that I would prefer not to be sick, wet, cold or frightened. He assured me that none of these circumstances were likely to happen. In the event, Florida failed to live up to its reputation; the first three states certainly occurred and the fourth was a near thing. Nick now intends to sail the boat to Antigua, where warmth and sun, calm seas and palm-shaded beaches might lure me out, if invited, for another try.

In Plymouth, Grammar Schools still existed. Pinks went to Devonport High, making long-lasting friendships, and from there to Durham University to read geography. While there she became Captain of Women's Rugby – an unlikely position for a slender individual of about eight stone in weight and five feet four tall. Knocked out by heftier folk on the field of battle, she missed part of a term at university but managed a degree and went on to teacher-training at Homerton College in Cambridge. Talented, capable and lovely – as the unbiased grandmother of a first grandchild, I am allowed to say such things – she went on to become Head of geography at the College of South Dartmoor, a State school judged 'Outstanding' by Inspectors. The then headmaster retired, trailing clouds of glory.

Pinks had been there for seven years. With the arrival of a new Headmaster of the New Broom variety, unsettling changes occurred across the board. It was time for her and, indeed, several other colleagues, to move on. By chance she saw an advertisement; Badminton School near Bristol – a girls' Public School – was in the market for a Head of geography. We all considered that Pinks was tailor-made for the post. Very sensibly, so did Badminton. She joined in the autumn term, 2011.

She blossomed in the new environment, could walk to the school from her flat in Bristol in seven minutes and was determined to become so indispensible to the school that, in spite of the post being nominally only for the period of her predecessor's maternity leave, the headmistress would find it hard to let her go.

27

Charlotte

Charlotte trained as a social worker, padding about the streets of Tower Hamlets with a youthful innocence that somehow kept her safe in those shabby haunts. After a series of smitten young men had been disposed of, she met Spencer Maizels while playing tennis. He had graduated from Cambridge where he had done well and had won a Kennedy Scholarship to Harvard. Now he was in the City, ambitious, clever and a rising star. They were married a month after Nick and Bids' wedding – it was a busy summer – and made their home in London. Their eldest son, James, was born five years later, twenty-four hours after his cousin Christopher, Nick's second child.

After James's birth in '82, Lucy was born just after Christmas '84 and Tom in August '88. Spencer was forging ahead in the City and formed, with a colleague, his own investment company, Maizels Westerberg. The little family lived first in Chepstow Place in Notting Hill, and then, as the family enlarged, moved to a bigger house in Chepstow Villas.

Maggie, who had originally been engaged to do some cleaning, became very much part of the family but it was soon clear that, had she been blessed with a proper education, she could have run any large international corporation, or even a small country, with very little trouble. The Maizels family benefited from the fact that she was *not* running a corporation or a country of any size and could concentrate her energies on them.

Lucy gave every indication, early on, of owning a pretty firm character. She had been breast-fed from birth and when the time came for a gradual weaning onto a bottle she resolutely refused, with pursed lips, such a substitute for the real thing. Charlotte struggled with the problem.

"Go out for the day," said Maggie at last to Charlotte, "and leave her to me."

Reluctant but exhausted, Charlotte departed.

She found on her return that, rather than starve to death, Lucy had unenthusiastically given in to a will-power even stronger than her own and would grudgingly now accept the occasional bottle.

Dramas suited Maggie. Much later, they moved to the new house before it was ready and lived for some weeks in its dusty basement while work went on overhead. Charlotte was pregnant with Tom. Maggie got them through this demanding time and into calmer waters, becoming indispensable the while. Later, when with quiet authority she said to the children, "Pack up your toys now, its time for bed," everyone packed up their toys and proceeded upstairs – no shouting from her, no whining from them – and got into the bath.

Spencer, with his good brain and abilities, advanced in his career as a Merchant Banker. Almost everything he had achieved in his life had prospered and turned to gold, and the disease with which he was diagnosed in the spring of '93 was certainly, in his mind, not going to be the exception to this rule. For almost twenty months he fought gallantly against gastric carcinoma, in denial as to its probable, and indeed eventual, outcome. The children were ten, seven and four years old when he became ill, some of their childhood clouded, therefore, by this long-drawn-out drama, the exhaustion of their mother and the death of their father at the age of forty-three.

Zita, a New Zealand Maori, came to the family as an *au pair* for several years over the time of Spencer's illness. She was imperturbable and unflappable in this complex and difficult period.

Tom, with the unthinking outspokenness of a very young child, once said chattily to Zita over lunch, "You're rather ugly, Zeet babe." Zita was not in the least offended. "That's not a very nice thing to say, Tom," she replied calmly. "Now, hurry up and eat your pudding." She eventually returned to New Zealand but has remained in contact ever since.

Charlotte and Spencer were negotiating to buy Cley Hall, a large and beautiful eighteenth century house on the north Norfolk coast, at the time of his diagnosis. "Will you go ahead with the idea?" I asked him, expecting the answer, 'probably not'. He looked astonished.

"Of course," he said. 'Why ever not?' He must have been thinking, 'I'm going to beat this disease and I've always wanted a country house.' So the purchase went ahead in spite of the situation and twenty months later the family spent his last Christmas there when it was all too clear that he had not long to live. They went back to London in the early New Year.

I was booked to go skiing in the third week of January '95 and was due to spend a night at their house before flying out to France. Some unexplainable feeling prompted me to abandon the skiing but to go to London anyway.

"I'm not going to France," I told Charlotte as I arrived, "and I can't be persuaded since I haven't brought any ski kit."

"Oh, Mummy," she said, looking exhausted, "this has been going on for weeks and it'll be ages before you're needed."

Over that weekend, six different doctors came to the house. Not one knew anything about Spencer's condition, diagnosis or prognosis. Each one had to be told the whole story. One of them ordered diamorphine and I went at midnight by taxi through the brightly lit streets of the West End to fetch it from an all-night chemist, with a heightened sense of the life-and-death drama going on silently at home, while the night-life of London surged unconcernedly and loudly on. Another of the doctors said briskly, "I'm going to take him into hospital – otherwise he's going to die."

"He's not going anywhere," replied Charlotte firmly. He died later that night, at home. The twelve-year-old James insisted on being present in the room at his father's death.

This tragedy had a profound effect on the children and Charlotte. She was left to make the important immediate decision about the next school for James. He was about to leave The Hall Prep School in Hampstead. Spencer, who had been educated at Harrow Grammar School, had wanted what he regarded as the best education for his elder son and had chosen Eton. But in the same year as his father's death, was it right for James to leave home and go to a boarding school for the first time? Charlotte decided that it was not.

He went to Westminster School, did well and proceeded in due course to St Edmund's Hall in Oxford where he read Economics and Business Studies. From there he followed the example of his father and joined the City, being recruited first by the American bank, Merrill Lynch. Some five years later, exhausted and over-worked, he left Merrill and joined Deutsche Bank. He was considerably happier here and thrived in the appreciative atmosphere.

The children when small all went, in turn, to Mrs Mynor's Nursery School, just up the road from their house. The young Princes were there too, William coinciding with James and Harry with Lucy.

"Will you come and have lunch?" Harry asked Lucy. She was duly delivered to Kensington Palace by Charlotte, and I was to collect her afterwards. I mounted the grand staircase and found the children playing on the large landing at the top and the nanny hovering.

"What did you have to eat?" I asked Lucy as we drove home.

"We had banana custard," she said scornfully, "and it was disgusting."

Lucy's time at Pembridge Hall Girls' School, in Notting Hill, was not happy. A teacher remarked to Charlotte that Lucy was "very average, Mrs Maizels, very average". We were all well aware, even at her tender age, that 'average' was not an adjective we recognised to describe Lucy, then or ever. Quite soon she moved to Trevor-Roberts School in West Hampstead and within a month had been awarded a morale-raising prize. Just before she left, aged thirteen, the headmaster – a wonderfully eccentric character – introduced her to a Governor of the school saying, "This is my Head Girl and they don't come much better!" She followed her brother to Westminster for her A levels and became a Medical Student at Bristol.

In her fourth year she took a separate degree in International Medicine, since her ambition then was to join *Médicins sans Frontières*, or Merlin, the British equivalent, and work abroad. She had many adventures during the vacations; working in Indonesia, she returned with Dengue fever, was admitted to the Bristol Royal Infirmary and found that being a patient gave her a very different and frustrating view of the NHS from that of a medic. In July 2009, she qualified as a junior doctor and began her first job at St George's Hospital in Tooting.

During her second job, (2010/11) now a senior houseman at Frimley Hospital, she took unpaid leave for a month and raced another team, with many icy adventures, to the magnetic North Pole! Hating being cold, let alone freezing, I would give quite a lot of money *not* to do such a thing whereas Lucy paid quite a lot to *do* it.

Next, in 2011, now fully qualified and taking a year off, she whizzed out to Costa Rica as one of the leaders attached to an Operation Raleigh International Expedition. Three months later, just in time for Christmas, she arrived back to regale us all with tales of the adventures of the youngsters of whom she had been in charge. For many of them it had been a life-changing experience and Lucy herself had learnt much about being a leader.

The only one of the three to go to boarding school was, by his own choice, Tom. He went to Oundle near Peterborough in the Midlands. Charlotte let him go with difficulty and missed him badly but it quickly became evident that this had been one of the best decisions that she had made. It suited him perfectly. Head of House, Captain of this team, President of that Society, DJ on the internal radio shows and with a circle of delightful friends, he can be said to have made a great success of his time there. He was offered a place at Bristol University to read History and French on condition that he got three As at A level. This was a challenge to which he rose triumphantly – succeeding by sheer hard work and determination.

Three years in Bristol (two coinciding with Lucy) and an enjoyable one at the University of Bordeaux, were followed by a well-deserved First Class Honours degree. My minuscule input towards this wonderful result was to search through his excellent dissertation on *The Role of the Newspapers in the Suez Crisis* for split infinitives and eliminate them.

During his last summer vacation, Tom undertook some work experience with a small 'boutique' investment bank specialising in Mergers and Acquisitions. At the end of his three weeks work the director phoned and asked him to come in. With some trepidation – "What have I done?" – Tom did so.

"We'd like to offer you a job," said the director. "Finish your degree, have next summer off and join us in September."

Charlotte has achieved a great triumph in bringing up her three children so successfully. Doing so alone was never going to be easy since all major decisions had to be hers and emotional recovery after Spencer's death had to be subordinated to that of the children. They and their education, their needs and lives and happiness have been foremost in her thoughts, decisions and actions ever since. Her reward is three hard-working, charming and useful young adults.

She has worked part-time for an affluent Church charity in London for some years, enjoying the rich variety of the clerical Trustees and being affectionately appreciated by them for down-to-earth common sense and sound judgement.

27

Simon

Simon was born in Malta in December 1957 and tagged along with our peripatetic life from there to Chatham, to Bath, to Chalton while David was Captain of *Mercury* and from there to Chatham again. From here he joined Horris Hill Prep School. One of his early letters poignantly informed us that he was 'just OK'. But we were off to Singapore and had no option for him but a boarding school.

From there he went to Marlborough College where he became, in time, Head Boy of Summerfield House. In his last term the house master took a sabbatical and was replaced temporarily by a pleasant but rather less competent character. It more or less fell to Simon to keep the house going, which he did as well as coping with A levels.

In spite of being both a son and grandson of the Navy, he wanted to be a pilot. Looking back, it is obvious that flying, all his life, had been his aspiration. He had made endless model aircraft as a child, had joined the air section of the school training corps and completed a gliding course.

For a very brief while he contemplated flying helicopters. "Those machines are out to kill you," he said after being taken on a demonstration run, and went off the idea. The RAF generously awarded him a flying scholarship which enabled him to achieve his Private Pilot's Licence at Goodwood. After that he was even more determined to be a commercial pilot. The generosity, however, was spoilt by the news that a slight heart anomaly had shown up on his ECG.

"Do not consider a career as a pilot," said the RAF. "We certainly wouldn't let you join as one."

Horribly downcast and depressing to live with, he found a job cutting the hedges of Hampshire and another working in a golf club. Finally a village friend, the chief engineer of Concorde, could stand the grumbling no longer.

"Go to the Civil Aviation Authority and have yourself done over by the doctors there," he advised. "They will tell you whether to forget flying or not."

The verdict, fought for kindly and convincingly by a distinguished physician at the CAA, was that he could see no reason why the slight heart anomaly should prevent a career as a pilot. (It became clear, much later, that all three of my children had the same insignificant irregularity, which caused none of them the slightest inconvenience. Who had passed it on, David or I?)

Equally fortunately, in 1979 Simon gained a place at Hamble where, in those days, British Airways trained their pilots. David and I took him there and were just settling him into his room when a young man, a fellow student, appeared at the door.

"Hi, I'm Richard. Who are you?" he enquired. They became and remain the best of friends to this day.

"I should like you all to understand," said the tutor on the first day of the two-year course, "that behind every one of your sixteen chairs, are a hundred people wishing they were sitting there."

Having trained them at vast expense as Commercial Pilots, BA then announced that it had no further use for them. Simon went to South Africa and found a job flying single-engine aircraft from Johannesburg to Durban, over the Drakensberg Mountains, sometimes in great danger both to himself and his passengers. At times he navigated by peering over the side at the passing landscape. David and I longed for his letters but found that most of them brought news of fresh near, or actual, disasters – 'run out of money' or 'nearly flew into a mountain' or 'almost got lost in the desert but luckily recognised a certain bush'.

It was a great relief when his great friend Richard, the fellow ex-Hamble student, wrote to him to say that British Midland Airways had begun recruiting. Simon came home and joined. A few years later he transferred to British Caledonian. This was then swallowed by BA. He was back in the fold again, flying 747 400s on long-distance flights to far-flung parts of the world, becoming a Captain in 2001.

Sally Boysen was a flight attendant with British Caledonian and was also scooped up into BA. She had taken some banking exams before joining the airline but till then, apart from these, had few qualifications. She and Simon met in 1985 through their work and married in 1988, attended by Pinks and Lucy, aged ten and three as bridesmaids and Christopher and James who were six. Tom, aged three months, was also present at the wedding but took no part in the proceedings apart from raising his voice occasionally.

They lived at first in Jasmine Cottage, a tiny house in a hamlet near Horsted Keynes in West Sussex. Simon at that time flew conveniently from nearby Gatwick. (Now he flies from Terminal Five at Heathrow, the M25 taking longer and longer to negotiate.)

A year or so later, Sally gave consideration to her job as a BA stewardess. 'There must be more to life than this,' she thought. She was admitted to Sussex University, not far from where they lived, and read Law for three years. Simon phoned me with the result of her Finals.

"Sally just missed a Second," he said. Awkwardly, I composed as comforting a reply as possible. "Oh, well, a Third is not too bad."

"No, no," he said, laughing. "I was teasing. She got a First!"

She went on to become a solicitor, worked for American Express and in due course became pregnant. They came to visit. "Would you mind sitting down," they said, "you're in for a shock. We're having twins."

Not many twins had occurred in any of our families before. Anna and Jack duly arrived on 5th April 2000 by Caesarean section. Possibly, during their first six months, Sally might have thought wistfully of sending them back whence they came, had such a thing been possible, but slowly life became easier. By the time they were two, she was seeing friends coping again with the sleepless nights and nappies of their second child, while her two were progressing splendidly into small people with the controversial help of Gina Ford's *The Contented Little Baby Book*. (Some people turn purple with fury at the very name of G Ford, accusing her of being far too prescriptive and rigid in her 'rules', but many of her suggestions, if not followed too closely or inflexibly, are useful and effective. Certainly they worked for the twins.)

I gave Sally a subsequent book, *Toddler Taming* by Dr Christopher Green. 'Toddlers come in all forms of life, from the little angel to the urban guerrilla and they are all normal,' it proclaimed. (I have the next title lined up for her, well in advance of teenagery, entitled *Divas and Door-Slammers* by Charlie Taylor. They are, though, such delightful children that both they, and the rest of us, are hopeful that this particular stage of life will pass with good humour and without too much door-slamming.)

The twins – or 'Twiglets' – as Charlotte nicknamed them, are the only grandchildren of Sally's mother, Doreen.

She lives not far away and they are the true focus of her energy and concern. Sally became a hard-working Governor of their first school, Fonthill Lodge, and, when they were eleven, they moved on to separate schools – Anna to Burgess School for Girls and Jack to Brighton College.

With a wise look at what the world may be like in the middle distance, Jack's school prescribes Mandarin as a compulsory subject. With Spanish as well, Jack, when adult, is likely to be able to communicate with about 75% of the population of the globe. Already, after one term, as they pass a Chinese restaurant on the way home, he is able to give it an English name.

28

Going to Gokyo

The paper pants proved not to be a good idea. The designer had clearly not envisaged the immersion of his product in a waist-deep river several times in one day. Packets of Ryvita suffered much the same fate. They had been amongst the articles that, too late, we discovered not to be essential for walking in the eastern foothills of Nepal.

My sister Camilla and I exchanged our husbands, our adult children and our normal occupations for a strenuous trek. This brought us from the warmth of the flat Terai in the south to the icy cold of the Himalayan Mountains in the north. In spite of the ravishing beauty of this part of the country, there were no other tourists. (Later, we quite understood why.) Three local porters carried the gear, their English no more fluent than my Nepali. I carried a book of vocabulary along the river valleys and into the high hills, learning nouns and verbs as I went along.

Many nights were spent in small village tea-houses. On catching sight of the first of these, Camilla rejected it out of hand. "I am not staying in a chicken-infested, dog-infested, probably rat-infested hovel, with half the population of the village squatting round, gazing in," she informed me and our retainers. They had begun to unload the conical wicker baskets in the hope that our day's journey was at an end.

"All are same, *Memsahib*," said our head porter, repacking the *dokas*. "If want private you bring tent." But Camilla was off, striding into the middle distance. At the next village, he smiled smugly. "See, *Memsahib*?" He spoke with quiet satisfaction, "All same."

Not quite the same. In addition to the disadvantages of the first *bhatti*, this one, I discovered, was bedbug-infested as well. Two wooden tables became our beds; overhead was a bamboo ceiling on which the *bhatti*-keeper, his wife, his mother and numerous children slept. The porters cooked our supper over a fire on the floor, the smoke of which blew straight into our eyes. Incongruously, Camilla's tape recorder came into its own as a Mozart Piano Concerto lilted out to a mystified audience of *Memsahib*-watchers sitting outside in the dark. The only light was from the fire and a few candles and we felt further back than the Middle Ages.

After dark, from neighbouring huts arose what we later accepted as the normal nocturnal noises of Nepalese villages. Dogs barked, hens cheeped, goats 'baa'ed, babies cried, people sang, chatted, coughed, spat and, eventually, snored. I was scratching bites. Next morning, after a sleepless night, we seriously wondered if we could manage a further three weeks of similar nights and remain reasonably sane. Luckily, things improved. Our spirits rose.

We waded across the same winding river seventeen times in one day. Occasionally the bottom was relatively flat, sometimes it consisted of large rounded boulders, pregnant with imminent disaster. Usually it was waist-deep and flowing strongly. In the hot sun, clothes dried off between the immersions, except for the paper pants which had to be abandoned in favour of the more robust sort.

Days of walking on high narrow paths cut into the sides of cliffs or along hot dusty trails up and down enormous hills followed. Going down was almost as taxing as climbing up and it was with trepidation that we wondered if we were about to suffer from '*Memsahib's* Knee'. Where there *were* bridges, sometimes over foaming torrents far below, they were interesting but not for the faint-hearted. Many of the wooden slats were missing or loose and a rather dismaying swaying motion occurred as one crossed. It was best not to hover on the brink but to step straight onto the bridge before the nerves shredded.

Many of the slopes were terraced into tiny fields and irrigated to grow rice and vegetables. People were friendly and curious. "How old are you?" was a favourite question. At one house, we encountered the mother of a retired Gurkha sergeant. She squatted on a mat in the sun in her long, brightly coloured skirt, rubbing the corn off maize cobs and clearly ruling the roost. Astonishment at our sudden appearance added further lines to her brown face. Long earrings quivered with disapproval as she let out a stream of startled words. Her son interpreted her displeasure.

"She say, 'Why you tramping through the hills with no man?'" (Evidently the porters didn't count.) "She say, 'Why you not at home, cooking your husband's rice and husking your maize?'" A long explanation was beyond my grasp of the language. Slightly chastened, we resumed our tramping.

From a high track, the view of the mountains was sometimes obscured by clouds like teased-out cotton wool, giving glimpses of snowy peaks, loftier than any imagination could have foreseen, shining icily white through the misty veil. We were entering a landscape of immense scale and drama. Huge soaring griffon vultures circled slowly overhead. Nearer to hand, exotic butterflies and unfamiliar birds darted from bush to bush.

At nearly 12,000 feet, Namche Bazaar is the busy start-point for many expeditions going on to climb Everest or at least reach the Base Camp. We had no such ambition. We aimed to climb to the lesser peak and lakes of Gokyo. We acquired a gnarled and smiling Sherpa guide, Penuri. He instructed us, "You must hire down-clothes for very cold. I have yak and two tents, will take food for week."

The deserted path up to Gokyo was high above the Dudh Kosi River. On the first evening, Camilla complained of a persistent headache. Nothing would shift it – she was clearly suffering from altitude sickness and the only safe course of action was to descend. Reluctantly she walked back down with a guide to Syangboche and its Trekkers' Lodge.

I felt sad for her but we decided I should go on as arranged, so Penuri, the yak and I climbed further up the snow-filled valley to a series of large milky-turquoise lakes, the source of the great river which we had encountered for much of our journey.

As we walked, Penuri remarked casually that a yeti inhabited these regions. "Girl tending yaks was attacked, thrown in river. Three yaks killed, one eaten. Happen here." He pointed out the exact spot where the terrible event had occurred. In this desolate and bleak landscape, disbelief was suspended. A colossal footprint in the snow would have come as no surprise.

The solitary huts of Gokyo lay by the last green lake, circled by dizzy heights. I toiled alone up Gokyo Ri – a gruelling struggle to the 18,000 foot summit. The reward for this mighty effort of will was a superb prospect of the surrounding massive mountains, gleaming with brilliant gold and flame in the sunset. Clouds of powdered snow were swept off the pinnacles by a high wind from Tibet. A glacier tumbled off them, bluey-green. I tottered down to where Penuri had prepared supper and then, in my tent, spent the coldest night of my life in spite of wearing every available garment.

The next day was cloudless, with sparkling sunshine

which transformed the top lake from freezing grey to an impossible green. Crossing the glacier we emerged on the other side of the valley. I strode on alone, ahead of Penuri and the yak, over close-cropped grass with the young river singing beside me, physically fitter than I was ever likely to be again, in ravishing cold air and brilliant sun which vied with each other to provide the perfect shirt-sleeve temperature. The sky was bluer than gentians and a bird soared silently on wide wings between the enclosing mountain ridges. After the climax of yesterday's achievements and enraptured by my surroundings, I experienced one of those rare moments of entire and perfect happiness, brief but unforgettable.

Camilla and I were reunited at Tyangboche on its peaceful hill with its famous Monastery, and Penuri, like a nut-brown nanny, was relieved to have his two charges together again.

Before flying home, we had booked one night at the Everest View Hotel, the highest in the world. Snowed in by mighty storms, however, we and a dozen other guests were trapped for a week like the cast of an Agatha Christie play – without the murders.

Daily and hopefully we tramped down to the airstrip. Increasingly glumly, we trudged back up again. Taking off at last from the minute airstrip was terrifying. One felt it would be all too easy to flip over the edge at the end of the runway and land in the Dudh Kosi, some 1000 feet below. In the event, we took a firm grip of our twanging nerves, whizzed away over the melting snow, turned sharp right to avoid a mountain and landed, somewhat relieved, an hour later in Kathmandu.

29

Siblings

Our father bestowed nicknames on each of his daughters, which, in Diana's case, remained with her for life, at least as far as the family was concerned. Tucked into her cradle as a small baby, he thought she looked like a winkle in its shell. I will continue to refer to her as Diana, but Winkie or Wink is her 'proper' name in the family. Mine was Juggins or Jug but no-one explained why and no-one called me that except my parents. Camilla's nickname was Muggleton – an equally inexplicable choice – which faded from use quite early. She was invariably called Milla.

Diana hid her strength of character behind a gentle and non-confrontational exterior and endured considerable bullying both from our mother and, later, from our headmistress, Matt. She trained as a Norland nurse and worked in a nursery before marrying Peter, the future vicar, acquiring thereby a protector for life. They had five children – Tim, the clever, musical and artistic polymath and atheist, David, another vicar, Caroline, a further artist with one son Tom, Victoria who qualified as a nurse, married and had four children but was widowed by the far too early death of her excellent husband, David Turner, and Matthew, the youngest, who made a name for himself as a video maker, working for such prestigious companies as BA and the London Library.

Peter moved parishes a couple of times, ending up in Lutterworth in the Midlands. A country neighbour, a landed-gentleman's wife, remarked, "It is *so* convenient – only two hours from Harrods."

Diana was a loyal and supportive clergy wife. Had she been married to a less conservatively-clerical husband, I feel she would have been almost as questioning of her faith as I became, notwithstanding our clergy ancestors and traditional Church of England upbringing. Books by Don Cupitt, of *Sea of Faith* fame, and other works by non-theists were openly on her bookshelves.

She suffered a sub-arachnoid haemorrhage quite suddenly one afternoon and was in Leicester hospital in a coma for several days. Naturally, the whole parish was prevailed upon to pray for her recovery. According to Peter, that this was eventually achieved was entirely due to these prayers. The doctors who finally operated and thus relieved the pressure were obviously doing no more than acting as God's agents. What, I wondered, about all the people in the world who have no-one to pray for them? Will God take no notice of them unless nudged by the faithful? Does God need to be told what's needed before he acts? Is he able to step in and tweak the Laws of Nature for those fortunate enough to be prayed for?

After her recovery and in their retirement, Diana and Peter moved to a nearby village. They filled the next few years with good works, and then returned to a new house in Lutterworth. Gradually it became apparent that Peter was losing his memory. It is true to say that he had been her rock. Now she gallantly bore the burden of his progressive illness. Over the years, it steadily sapped her strength and few knew how heavy the load proved. She died peacefully in her sleep, in October 2009, leaving the problem of Peter to their supportive adult children.

Camilla, my younger sister, was sent to the Godolphin School in Salisbury. Either Matt had drawn the line at welcoming yet another Rosedale sister to Calne or the thought of dealing with Matt for a further five years had been too much for our parents. Camilla, with her strong character, tested the patience of her long-suffering house-mistress but remained in warm touch for many years. Matt, who much preferred those who stood up to her, would have enjoyed the tussles.

She married early, aged twenty, partly to escape from home where she and our mother were sometimes loudly at loggerheads, being far too alike for comfort.

Three boys and one girl were born. Mark, the eldest, just a few months older than Nick, went into the Modern Art world, working for several years in Pittsburgh, Philadelphia and later his wife, Sheena, was Curator at Tate Modern in London. The second, Anthony, (always known as Nutty and owned by a dog called Fruit when grown-up) became a teacher in Twyford Prep School, near Winchester. Pip was the only daughter. She married and had two girls, Abigail and Harriet. Ben, an international lawyer working mainly in the USA, was the youngest of Camilla's children.

Camilla had qualified in Institutional Management, a tremendous advantage when it was her turn to cook for the fellow overland-travellers when she and I journeyed, dramatically, from Victoria Station to Kathmandu. Her meals were much preferred to those produced by Fred, the statutary hippy, and his girlfriend. Their offerings tended to be either raw or burnt.

Sadly divorced, eventually, from Michael Francis, Camilla had worked at the Princess Alice Hospice in Esher as the Volunteers' Organiser. When she retired from this she moved to Chichester. It was good to have her living closer and we saw a good deal of each other. Ben, working in

Washington DC, had become engaged to, and married, an American fellow lawyer, but the marriage was unhappy and they were divorced within two years. Much later he met, and became happily engaged to, the delightful Leslie Ellis and they were married in the spring of 2012.

Camilla was unfortunate enough to become ill round about Christmas 2006, when it seemed that all the world of Chichester had flu. It was assumed by one and all that she also had flu. In reality and disastrously she did not. The doctors were run off their feet, those who reluctantly visited being of the opinion that here was a woman making far too much fuss, her painful abdomen being the result of constipation. They prescribed aperients and left. Taken in by this lack of concern at her condition, I had said to her daughter, Pip, only a day or two earlier, that I was sure she'd be better soon and that flu wasn't usually a fatal illness.

I spent a night with Camilla at her house in Chichester over the New Year. There was no change in her condition and she thanked me and suggested that I should go home and we would keep closely in touch. A phone call woke me early the next day, 2nd January.

"Please come, I feel terrible."

"I'm on my way," I said.

There was no answer to the door bell which I pressed several times. I had noticed a police car lurking on a traffic island nearby and I explained to the young policeman why it was essential that I should get into the house.

"Wait at the front door and I'll go round the back and see if I can get in," he said. I waited, palms sweaty with fear and apprehension. He managed to find a way into the small back garden, broke a downstairs window, climbed in and opened the door. We went upstairs. Camilla was lying dead on the landing.

A thousand terrible emotions grabbed me, chiefly severe

shock, an almost physical pain, grief, anger that whatever had killed her had been totally undiagnosed and unexpected, and horror at the thought that at this moment only I, of all the family, knew what had happened and that I would have to tell them.

Authority, in the guise of the young police officer, flowed seamlessly into action. He sent for a doctor, an ambulance arrived, the window was mended and they all went away. I sat alone in her kitchen in a state of complete devastation and shock, trying to stop shivering, utterly appalled. Eventually, still shaking, I phoned Michael, Camilla's former husband, and we agreed that he would phone his son-in-law David at work, so that he could rush home and break the news to Pip as gently as such dire information can be given. Before this could happen, the phone rang.

"Mum?" said Pip, anxiously. "How are you?" Even our father had had difficulty deciding which of his daughters was speaking to him on the phone and Pip had not distinguished my voice from her mother's. I had to tell her what had happened. It was one of the most dreadful and haunting experiences of my life.

At *post mortem*, Camilla was found to have had an undiagnosed internal bleed – a ruptured mesenteric aneurism. (This is the rupturing of an already dilated blood vessel.) We should probably have laid complaints about her treatment, or lack of it, but as nothing would have altered the tragedy, we didn't.

Barney, born in 1936, was the longed-for son, the brown-eyed little boy, the only brother, who replaced Camilla as the youngest child after her six pleasant years in that capacity. She kept a pretty strict watch on this usurper of her position. This probably saved him from being spoilt and idolised by all and sundry. He was three when the war began and was carted about on our evacuation-perambulations as we avoided the possible bombs of suburbia. He was about nine when peace of a kind broke out but his childhood was clouded, like ours, by the dark shadows of war. After his day-prep school in Wimbledon, he went off to Stowe School in Buckinghamshire, where, amongst other distinctions, he was appointed Head Boy and was an excellent Frederick in *The Pirates of Penzance*. It was while he was doing his National Service that he found himself in Iraq, saved someone from bleeding to death and decided to become a doctor. St Thomas's trained him, and he worked in Nigeria and later in Nepal. He and a few other doctors and nurses drove there overland and set up the Britain-Nepal Medical Trust (BNMT.) This aimed to improve the health of the people of eastern Nepal, where TB was endemic and, eventually, to hand over to local medical staff.

After a year, in 1969, he flew home for his wedding to Rachel Cripps, grand-daughter of Stafford Cripps. David and I were in Singapore at the time so we missed the rain-soaked ceremony in Gloucestershire. Together they spent the next three years working on the East/West Highway in Nepal, vaccinating such young as they could persuade to have the anti-TB injections, treating patients in the somewhat rudimentary hospital in Biratnagar on the Terai and striding about the foothills training local people to provide simple remedies for the more usual non-fatal maladies of their small communities. The Britain-Nepal Medical Trust thrives to this day.

The life suited them perfectly; they spoke the language fluently and had friends not only amongst the Nepalese people but made long-lasting friendships with fellow workers. I visited them from the naval base in Singapore, meeting my new sister-in-law for the first time.

In 1972 they wended their way home circuitously and pregnant with Rupert, via Everest Base Camp. They made their home in Marlborough where Barney became a GP (in the practice occupied for four generations by the famous Doctors

Maurice) and where Rupert and three other young Rosedales, Lawrence, Ben and Kath, were born and brought up.

There is a dramatic photograph of Barney crossing the Icefall, far above Everest Base Camp. As the doctor, he had joined the 1972 expedition, led by Chris Bonington, which was sadly unsuccessful in its attempt to reach the summit. The weather defeated them.

In Marlborough, Barney and Rachel became important and active members of the rich life of the town and the many activities of the College. Not only was he a busy GP but was also the doctor for the College, dealing with the Marlborough boys and, after girls were admitted, with these too. Rachel had trained as a teacher and was much occupied with setting up pre-school and nursery facilities in the town. Later she qualified as a Counsellor and had an active practice based in Swindon, combining this with the doings of their large family and much welcoming hospitality to a great many friends.

They are both active members of the Quaker community. I find the hour of silence, when occasionally I go with them to a Meeting, to be a wonderful temporary withdrawing from the busy world. I enjoy the time given for unhurried thinking and attempts at meditation and find it so different from the apparent uneasiness in the C of E of allowing anything longer than a few seconds of silence to occur.

Marlborough became twinned with a village in the Gambia and they are both much involved with this connection, as are many others in the town, travelling there often and helping the inhabitants improve the condition of their school, the water-supply and other amenities and to take over the enhanced governance of the village. Marlborough youngsters in their gap-year are encouraged to spend part of it usefully there and young people from the African village are welcomed to Marlborough for short stays in local homes including Thornsend.

30

Harting

David would have retired in 1970, had he not been selected, as the most senior Captain in the Royal Navy, to organise all the more junior Captains' appointments. This gave him a further five years at the Admiralty in a job which he loved and excelled in. He was the kind of sincere person who, totally charmingly, could convince an unwilling and sceptical naval officer that he had been personally selected by the First Sea Lord as the only individual capable of, say, the ultra-important (but extremely boring) task of towing some vessel from Portsmouth to Hong Kong.

(I find it interesting that, for the last fortnight of his naval career, in April 1975, he was paid at the proportional rate of ten thousand pounds a year. In the recent thirty-six years, the salary of a senior naval Captain has multiplied to about seven times this sum.)

Like King Solomon, who, when things were going badly, thought 'This will never end', and when they were going well, believed 'This will never last', David was inclined to pessimism. Solomon was given a ring on which was inscribed 'This too shall pass', a thought appropriate on all occasions, happy or sad. David asserted that he was a realist. My friend Grace called him Eeyore, after Pooh and Christopher Robin's donkey friend. Fortunately, we balanced each other perfectly since I am an optimist. I enjoy the prospect of things going right until they don't, while he had the misfortune to regard the future with anxiety until, to his surprise, it mostly turned out well.

David's father had, like his father before him, set the gentlest non-authoritarian pattern of parenthood, which he adopted in his turn. "Steady Right Down" (which eventually became "SRD" and had the same calming effect) uttered without a raised voice, was almost all that was needed to quench the sometimes over-exuberant noises and occasional squabbles of childhood and teenagery. This example has been followed, rewardingly, by the next generation.

We became part of village life. I joined the WI, making lasting friends (and avoiding being President by the skin of my teeth). I graduated from running the churchyard working-party to becoming the first ever female Churchwarden of Harting Church. It was an interesting but rather too long eight years. My first fellow warden retired and the second, Jack Masefield, nephew of the poet and an ex-war-prisoner of the Japanese, wanted, after several years, to do so too, after we had battled through an *interregnum*. I felt it wasn't fair on the new Rector to leave my post almost as soon as he had arrived and so the time stretched on. Women wardens are almost *de riguer* now but I could feel the long tale of history changing very slightly in the right direction on my appointment.

I was elected to the Parish Council and founded the Village Lunch Club. The idea for this came when I visited another Parish Council and discovered they had one. 'We could do that in Harting,' I informed myself and the Parish Council, 'only better.'

Not all innovations last long in Harting. This one has. Once a month anyone, young or old, can come to the Village Hall and have a home-cooked, usually hot, two course meal and coffee for a nominal amount. The cost in the mid-Nineties was £1.80 and it is now, a decade and a half later, still only £2.50.

Somehow, with the help of grants from the local District Council and other generous donations, we managed to buy a new oven, a plate-warmer and a commercial dishwasher. This last dealt with the washing-up of twenty-four plates, a trayful of glasses or most of the cutlery, in an astonishing two minutes per load. This lifted a huge burden. Some thirty to fifty people come each time, with even more at the festive Christmas lunch. The raffle keeps the finances on an even keel and three teams of cooks take turns to produce the excellent food. One of life's mysteries remains. This is that exactly the same recipe, cooked by each member of the team, can turn out so very differently from one chef to the next.

For some years I was the Controller of the WI Market in Petersfield. Only when 'Health and Safety' threatened to come and inspect our premises ('no dogs or washing machines allowed in the kitchen') did we put up two metaphorical fingers and close down. (Happily, 'H & S' have so far ignored the possibility of the Lunch Club poisoning its customers by having a dog in the kitchen when cooking the lunch.)

Harting was one of the first villages to have its own minibus. This goes to Chichester once a week, and to and from Petersfield with school children every term-time weekday, driven mostly by a rota of the mothers (thereby saving parents' time and petrol) and several times a week to Petersfield for shopping. For at least ten years, I drove the minibus once a fortnight, alternating with our great Chatham friend, Admiral John Parker, who had come to live in Harting. I also took over organising, for a while, the teas at the Harting Festivities from a splendid lady, Mrs Hosking, widow of a local farmer, whose riot-quelling hat (and character) kept disorder at bay.

In 1974, David was appointed 'Commander of the Most

Excellent Order of the British Empire' (or CBE for short) and retired a year later. (You are given a very pretty blue cross on a pink ribbon which you are supposed to wear round your neck on ceremonial occasions, which, after retirement, hardly ever occur.) He then became a useful member of the village. He was Chairman of the Royal British Legion, Chairman of the Cricket Club and for three years ran the Harting Festivities – an office requiring tact, diplomacy and sheer hard work.

A formidable lady named Mrs Frost, who was almost as wide as she was tall, ran the White Elephant Stall at this event. "Now, Cap'n," she declared the evening before, "you be down 'ere by five thirty tomorrer mornin', sharpish, with yer trailer an' take all me stuff down to that there field." Meekly, the distinguished naval Captain did as he was instructed. She was, of course, very soon 'eating out of his hand'.

Ten gallons of water for the teas was heated in a Soyer boiler, designed for the use of soldiers in the Crimean War more than a hundred years earlier. This had to be lit, with difficulty, in the morning and reached boiling point just in time for the afternoon teas. Bowling for the Pig, the Harting Mile Race, and other innocent entertainments brought the village together, to wander and chat and gossip over their tea and cakes.

At the end of the day, trailer-loads of rubbish were carted away to the dump by David, and Mrs Frost began collecting for the next year.

I woke one Saturday morning in late September, 1991, to find David in great abdominal pain. His doctor came and ordered an ambulance.

"I think you should send for your children," he said.

"Oh, they're all busy and working. I'm sure they couldn't come, and Simon has just flown to America," I rejoined, not yet understanding the situation.

"Nevertheless, I think you should try," he said firmly. "Let me talk to your son, Nick. He's a doctor, isn't he?"

Suddenly it was borne in on me that this was extremely serious.

I could hear him talking to Nick. "Your father has an aortic aneurysm and I fear it has ruptured," he said gently. "He will have to be operated on as soon as possible. I'm getting him into hospital now."

He put down the phone. "He asked me to tell you that he's on his way." Then, "Here's the ambulance. Let's get David in, then you and I will have a cup of tea and after that you can go down to St Richards."

I did as I was told but one of my life's regrets is that I didn't go with David in the ambulance. He was whirled away and the doctor left me in no doubt as to the gravity of the situation. I felt full of dread.

Sitting in the hospital visitors' waiting-room for hours, while an operation to try and repair the aneurysm was going on, I tried to read the newspaper. My brain was like a sieve – not a word settled there. Fears surrounded me, alternating with tremulous hopes.

Nick arrived from Plymouth and Charlotte from London. Simon joined us later, white and exhausted, after flying back from the United States.

David was in the Intensive Care Unit after the operation. We spent most of the time there but went back and forth between the hospital and home. During the next three days he seemed mostly asleep but roused occasionally. I phoned the Unit during the early hours of wakeful nights. There was 'no change'. Hearing me, Nick came in.

"It's no good," I acknowledged through tears. "He's not going to make it." It was difficult to take in the consequences in the new and lonely world opening like an abyss before us all. We hugged for comfort.

They turned off the life-support machine. We were all there holding his hands. How does one bear the moment when the light goes out, the breath stops and the other half of one's life has gone? With disbelief, pain, tears and difficulty.

After his retirement he had lived for sixteen years in South Harting, much loved and appreciated for his unobtrusive help around the village. In the church there were friends and family from far and wide, high and low, in every seat and with many standing, for a service celebrating his life.

Jean Yates, a retired Chief Wren Officer and a great friend, gave an address at this service. She spoke of David's "most endearing quality – his sheer unselfish unpretentiousness and generosity of spirit", and how successful and classless he was in his relationships with others. "Everyone who knew David speaks of his kindness, his courtesy, his interest in people and his self-effacement." She told an engaging story of how, after retirement, he, she and a full Admiral had all met in the signing-on queue at the local DHSS. "I doubt," she said, "if Petersfield had ever seen such a distinguished group. We waited with interest to see if we would be offered a job but I don't think any of us ever were."

A kind of numbness protects the very recently bereaved for a while and it seemed to me that I was the only person not in tears as I greeted people emerging after the service. Pain comes as the numbness wears off.

Just over a year later, I ventured to New Zealand with friends. We toured the two islands – four of us comfortably in a six-man campervan – and soon after we began our trip I had the only dream I ever had which featured David. He seemed so real, wearing his old tweed jacket, his arm round my shoulders. 'Wonderful,' I thought, 'so all this sorrow is in my imagination, and he hasn't died.' The reality, which hit me on waking, was hard to bear.

Lord Palmerston once said, "If I want a thing done well

in a distant part of the world, if I require a man with a good head, a good heart, lots of pluck and plenty of common sense, I always send for a Captain in the Royal Navy." This could have been said of David.

Harting Cricket Club had invited David to be their President, an honour he inherited from Alec Tyson, husband of my great friend, Grace. After David's death, and for some obscure reason, the Presidency passed to me. Watching the matches and attending the committee meetings brought me into enjoyable friendship with people in the village who I might otherwise not have known so well. I was President for seventeen years and finally resigned in 2008, ignoring cries of "You can't go – it's for life".

31

The Move to Pyramids

It was a difficult year after David died, compounded by a break-in at Noddswood while I was away for the weekend. I came back to find the front door damaged and precious things, like Nick's and Simon's twenty-first birthday grandfather clocks, missing.

"Would you like the Victim Support people to come and see you?" asked the policeman as he tried, and failed, to find finger-prints.

"No, thank you," I said, thinking myself far too independent to need any help. A charming woman came all the same, causing me, for the first time, to burst into unexpected tears of self-pity.

Noddswood was a mile out of South Harting, somewhat isolated, with no near neighbours. Now that I was alone, I needed to be in the village. It took me about a year to sell Noddswood and it was a wrench to leave a house where we had all been happy and the children had experienced their first real home.

Gillian Jacombe-Hood, a friend who was a secretary in the House of Commons, had built Pyramids in 1965 after her father died, in half an acre of the large garden of his house. A colourful and somewhat eccentric personality, Gillian had organised many people in the village into designing, stitching, stretching and sewing up a series of unique kneelers for the Church. They depict 'The Village and The Countryside' and are one of the glories of Harting Church and a fitting memorial to her.

She hated illness and all talk of it, so when she was diagnosed with a cancer, it was hardly mentioned and, mercifully, took very few weeks to kill her. Being a great gardener, Gillian had left the house to the Royal Horticultural Society. Her Will, somewhat naturally, rather miffed her relations. The RHS was only interested in the money which could be raised from the property. It was therefore no skin off her family's nose as to how much it was sold for and her brother advised me to offer the RHS £175,000, which they accepted.

Pyramids was designed by Patrick Litchfield, of the firm of Stroud and Litchfield, in London. It is such a unique house that photographs and articles about it appeared in several international architectural magazines and, in 1966, it was included in a book called *New Single Storey Houses*. (The word bungalow never crossed anyone's mind, let alone their lips.) Over thirty years later, English Heritage considered listing it as an 'interesting modern house' but by that time I had, fortunately, changed some of its less acceptable (to me) features and EH was no longer interested.

In 2010 when Harting, which was already in the new National Park, was being assessed as to which houses were to be included in the Conservation Area, I was surprised to find that Pyramids, once the object of a possible Listing, had been left out, while two ugly semi-detached houses next door were included (and have since been demolished). I was half annoyed, half pleased. Fortunately, this means that at least one layer of requests for permission to change anything can be ignored.

I turned the garage into another room with a big new window which looked out over the garden, and created an 'attic' in its pyramid roof for storage space. I had the slit windows in the kitchen enlarged so that I could see out without bending and all the twenty-eight-year-old sliding cupboard-doors were replaced. (Whatever one is looking for is always in the hidden part, I found.) A whole new kitchen came into existence as did a matching, pyramidically-roofed garage.

Part of the building had been a separate 'flat' (which I later integrated as part of the main house). This had been occupied by a lodger in Gillian's day so that someone would be living on the premises when she was in London during the week. Ronnie Valentine, escaping from a mutually unsatisfactory marriage, was one of these tenants. Later, he was invited into the main part of the house to occupy the single spare room (which he decorated with black wallpaper covered in multi-coloured flowers with curtains to match). He and Gillian became what she described as the 'Odd Couple'. Both were extremely cultivated, amusing and hospitable and travelled on many a holiday together.

The garden, which Gillian designed, was a delight to both of them. Ronnie was particularly good at suggesting new ploys, plants and plans and then sitting back languidly and watching others carry out the work. The Egyptian theme was maintained with two statues of the Sphinx and the yews were pruned to match the pyramid roofs. Indoors, a large mirror was commissioned that retained the same idea.

The large central room, with floor-to-ceiling windows looking east, south and west has, like all the rooms, an inside-pyramid-roof, only bigger than the others. Most of the available heat ascended into its apex. Sometime after I arrived I grew tired of heating the ceiling and commissioned a firm of marquee constructors to make a huge mattress of insulation and to hide it with a terracotta-coloured 'marquee' lining (though apparently it had to come with a hole in the middle for a possible pole). I called it being 'Pavilioned in Splendour'. Several billion dead flies are almost certainly lying peacefully and invisibly on this material. This fact disturbs me not at all. The room is certainly warmer, their small bodies possibly contributing in a minuscule way to the insulation.

The entire half-acre plot had originally been part of the orchard of a rectory (one of several in the village) some three hundred yards to the south. A circle of five or six large and ancient apple trees still survives to become one of the wonders of the garden. Their strangely pruned branches hang low enough to become a tree-climber's paradise (and much later, Jack, aged four, fell out of the oldest tree and broke his femur).

The view of the South Downs as they stride away to the east and south is spectacular. (The verb should now be 'was', since a great many trees have been planted to the south, hiding part of the aspect. No-one however, has a legal right to a view so nothing can be done about this.)

The alterations and repairs took some time. I rented a small flat in the village where I lived unhappily while the work dragged on for several weeks. When she built the house in 1965, Gillian had been advised to have under-floor electric central heating. "They're going to make electricity by nuclear fusion," she was told, "and it's going to be so cheap they won't be bothering you with any bills."

When this, predictably, failed to happen, she switched to storage heaters which I abandoned. Modern radiators heated by an oil boiler replaced these, backed-up by a wood-burning stove. Much later, I made an attempt to save the planet by having a solar panel to heat water installed on the roof. I shall be long under the ground before this pays for itself but it feels good, when luxuriating under a hot shower, that the water has been entirely heated, in the summer, by the sun. A further attempt at averting global warming by having Photovoltaic cells to make electricity mounted on the roof was thwarted by having too little space to erect more than five – an inadequate number to make the expense worthwhile.

Gillian had opened the garden annually under the National Gardens Scheme. After living in Pyramids for two years, I was persuaded by a gardening friend, Stephan Hopkinson, to carry on with this tradition. One of the visitors turned out to have been on the Planning Committee when the possible building of Pyramids came up for consideration. "It was such an unusual house," he said, "that I had to fight to get it passed; you'd never be allowed to build such a house now." As it has twenty-six outside walls, I was not surprised by this news.

I opened the garden enjoyably, under the same scheme, for a weekend in June for ten years. Then my gardener moved away to Yorkshire. It was too much work to continue to open. At last, a brilliant new gardener, Brian Dormer, entered my life and the garden flourished. (We opened it in the summer of 2010 in aid of Help for Heroes – a charity dealing with the problems of wounded British Servicemen returning from the on-dragging war in Afghanistan – a war which a long history of such skirmishes in that country foretells no such thing as victory.)

Peg Glue had been employed by Gillian Jacombe-Hood as a cleaner. She came every Wednesday, when Gillian was in London in the House of Commons, so saw very little of her employer. I was fortunate enough to inherit Peg with the house when I bought Pyramids. I regard her and her large extended family as the aristocracy of Harting. They have lived in the village for longer than most of the other inhabitants and she can remember when she and her many siblings were living with their parents in a two-bedroom cottage with no running water, no electricity and with the nightly visit of the 'Lavender Cart' collecting its load of human waste. She has become one of my most valued friends and stays, still on Wednesdays, far longer than she is paid to, during which time we have lengthy coffee-breaks to which Caroline Norman, my 'over-the-road friend', comes weekly to chat and catch up on all the local gossip. (Caroline, incidentally, gives frequent small evening parties where the guests sit round a long table on which generous food and even more generous wine is provided. Chat flows. I am lucky to live so near since I am always included.)

I bought nearly half an acre of the field that borders the garden on two sides. Borrowed sheep help to keep the grass mown and three hens, rescued from battery cages, potter about in hen heaven. Occasionally they get eaten by foxes and are then replaced. A corner of the field has become my kitchen garden or allotment. It produces sweet peas, runner beans, tomatoes, courgettes, rhubarb, lettuce, leeks, spinach, raspberries, rocket and other delicious delicacies.

I've lived in the village of South Harting for longer than I've have lived anywhere else – some forty-one years so far. It is the only village I've known intimately and thus I have little knowledge of other villages with which to compare it. People who have lived here for any length of time and then leave for whatever reason always seem to yearn to return. It's full of individuals with initiative – perhaps with rather more chiefs than Indians. We were one of the first villages to have a minibus and among the first to own our own shop. Major differences of opinion break out from time to time but appear to leave no lasting bitterness.

When some friends started a book group, the second book we tackled was *Middlemarch*, by George Eliot. During our subsequent discussion, it became apparent that affairs in small towns and villages haven't changed much in the century and a half since it was written. "Sounds quite like Harting," remarked one member. "There are still some awkward characters around to this day and most of us know almost everyone and their doings."

"You can't even sneeze," said another, "let alone develop any serious illness without someone who has heard about the occurrence on the grape-vine phoning to ask after your health and if they can do anything to help."

A village market was started by three of us in the Malthouse, one of the village halls. This opens for an hour on the first Friday of every month. Everything has to be home-produced, from cakes, savouries and other cooking, to honey, sweets, soups, cards, eggs, meat, vegetables, books, cider, knitting, sewing and silk scarves, pottery, jewellery, to chair-making, wood-work and plants. It has become, like the Lunch Club, an ongoing and popular occasion for people of the village, and those from further afield, to meet to buy fresh produce and have a chat over coffee and cakes. Its success meant that we outgrew the Malthouse and had to move up the road to the British Legion Hall, recently redecorated and no longer smelling of stale tobacco following the ban on smoking in public places. Health and Safety, that bugbear of initiative, hasn't, so far, caught up with us and demanded to inspect our kitchens, nor have we, as far as we know, killed off any of our customers. Village gardeners are catered for with three shows during the year, the prizes of a few pence and the occasional cup for the flowers and vegetables, fruit and cakes, eggs, flower-arrangements, photographs and honey being vied for passionately and prized far more highly than their intrinsic value. My friend Grace won the marmalade section year after year until she died. "Now," we said sadly, "we may have a chance to win."

191

32

Veterans Aid

It was with some trepidation that in 1995 I accepted an invitation to become a Trustee of a Service Charity. It had originally been set up in 1932 as the 'Embankment Fellowship Centre' (EFC) by Mrs Gilbert Huggins who, with her husband and young son had had the extreme good fortune to be rescued from drowning in Grand Harbour, Malta, after their motor boat was rammed and sunk. In gratitude for this almost miraculous escape she felt she must do something for the many impoverished post-First World War former Servicemen whom she saw everywhere on visits to London and who asked for help.

With other charities, Mrs Huggins organised a canteen and recreation room, a hostel and a night shelter, helping and housing many hundreds of destitute men who had served in the First World War and been abandoned to poverty and joblessness by a forgetful nation.

By 1969 the Charity had retained the initials EFC but renamed itself the 'Ex-Service Fellowship Centres' and, though still a small organisation, had continued with the good and much-needed work.

At the time I joined as a Trustee, urged into the role by a Harting friend, Brigadier John Ghika, the charity was still devoted to the ideals instilled by Mrs Huggins. John was the Chairman of the Council which consisted of about seven highly distinguished and mostly charming retired Service Officers across whose minds had passed the thought, possibly reluctantly, that in the middle of the 1990s, it might just be a good idea to have a woman as a fellow Trustee. My Service and nursing connections were a passport to the invitation to join the Council.

Meetings were held in a tiny office in Lower Grosvenor Place, hired at a much reduced rent from the owner, the Duke of Westminster. Later, we moved round the corner into Buckingham Palace Road to slightly larger premises, still a long way from the grandness of the address. In 2007 we changed our name again to Veterans Aid to reflect more closely what was actually being done.

VA has been described as the Accident and Emergency Service for veterans in crisis. It operates with a unique degree of independence and flexibility. Anyone who has been in any of the Services or the Merchant Navy, for however long or short a time, and of whatever rank, is eligible for immediate and practical help. The aid it gives is not a 'hand-out' but a 'hand-up', often from the depths of homelessness, debt, addiction, loneliness, relationship breakdowns, mental troubles or even prison.

These problems are not necessarily the result of having served in the Armed Forces. Early life-experiences, pre-service difficulties and poverty are often contributing factors. Veterans Aid staff are all ex-Service people and can make the troubled individuals who walk into the office still feel part of the Service family – veterans helping less fortunate veterans. Some 2,000 calls for help were dealt with during 2011, 20,000 nights of accommodation were provided and 150 street-dwellers were rehoused into sustainable homes.

VA's hostel in east London, New Belvedere House,

has fifty-nine rooms. Here the homeless are welcomed, (immediately if such is the need) and find in it a place of safety, often after miserable experiences on the streets. Each has his (and occasionally her) own comfortable bed-sitting room. Its aim is to enable people to 'get back to life', to regain health, self-respect and confidence and to progress gradually to independent living and if possible, through education and training, to jobs. On average they stay for nine months but, even when they have moved on, are still supported in the homes and work that they have been helped to find.

Slightly daunted at first by my isolation as the only woman, I began to pull my weight as I learnt the really excellent work which was being undertaken. The hostel was being renovated but, though the ground floor was provided with showers, there were no lavatories.

'They will just have to go up to the next floor' seemed to be the Council's general opinion. I was in a minority of one.

"They will pee in their washbasins," I maintained. There was a startled silence. When later the hostel was being enlarged with an extra floor, this omission was corrected.

Pat O'Connor, a remarkable woman, was originally the cleaner in the hostel. Several unsatisfactory managers came and, very soon, went and all the time Pat was not only cleaning but listening to people's troubles, encouraging them and giving good advice. We appointed her as the manager. It was an inspired move. The place is now run efficiently and as a very 'tight ship', with unbreakable rules about drink and drugs, but with loving care for each individual's needs. To her astonishment she was awarded a well-deserved MBE.

There was at one time a strong disagreement between the Trustees and the President. He had been much involved with the British Legion and, just before his retirement from VA, he proposed that it should be merged with the much larger Legion. He announced this as an almost as a *fait accompli* at the AGM without the Trustees having been informed. The British Legion is a huge and excellent organisation but it does not have the facility for the *immediate* intervention and practical help that is the guiding purpose and principle of VA.

I organised a revolt of the Trustees against this proposal with a letter to the President which we all signed. In it we warned that mass resignation would result if the threat of merging with the Legion was carried out. "Let 'em go," was reported to have been muttered by the President, but second (and better) thoughts prevailed and VA has gone on to be viewed as the leading charity for veterans in the UK.

I enjoyed the privilege of serving for twelve years on the Council, making lasting friendships with several of my fellow Trustees, and have since followed its progress with great interest. Any small annual profit made by the village market goes to chosen charities and one of these has been Veterans Aid.

33

Skiing

During our second time in Chatham in 1966, inspired by our friend Admiral John Parker, we took the children skiing in Andermatt in Switzerland. Marriage, producing children and moving about the world had prevented any further excursions to the slopes since my initial venture at the age of twenty-two. Even now, eighteen years later, boots were still attached to wooden skis with leather straps and a sort of curly spring held the ski onto the boot-heel. Skis themselves were enormously tall, measured to the standing height of an up-stretched arm and quite difficult to manoeuvre. In spite of this, this holiday bred in all the children a love of the sport which they have kept up ever since.

In the middle 1980s and for some twenty years, I was involved with a hilarious group of elderly skiers, termed by one of us the 'Order of the Zimmerai', which year after year kept the ski-slopes of France, Italy, and once, Austria, alive to the sound of laughter and occasional profanity.

This group evolved slowly and gathered speed – in two senses. Pip Calvert and Al Parker, a pair of long-standing friends, skied annually as a twosome, their wives declining invitations to sign up. Gradually, other folk asked if they might enlist and the total was about five when I joined in the fun. I was immediately persuaded to become the Secretary on the grounds that I was the only person who owned a computer at the time. Friends invited acquaintances, some suitable, some not (and these dropped out fairly fast) and after a few years the list of those who had, at varying times and however briefly, been honoured by membership of the Order, numbered an astonishing thirty-three persons.

On the last night of every skiing holiday we held an AGM, in one of the bedrooms of the hotel, co-chaired by Al and Pip, at which the Minutes of the last meeting of the Ancient, Honourable and Glorious Order of the Zimmerai were read by me. In 2004, some fourteen of the intrepid band were present. Six apologies had been received with such feeble excuses as that of Philip, 'gone to Antarctica in an attempt to improve his technique by watching penguins do it', or of Barry, 'not quite ready to rejoin after a heart op', or of another (quite different) Al, 'urgently recalled to Vienna – for a dinner party'. They were all in competition to be named, collectively, Wimps of the Week and were only beaten to this coveted position by an even more blatant rival, a description of whose triumph in this respect was to follow later.

The Minutes of the last meeting were received with the usual solemnity and duly signed as bearing some faint resemblance to what had actually occurred. Pip then gave a brief history of the Zimmerai, from the Dark Ages when he and Al had begun pottering about the slopes on wooden skis with spiral wire bindings, through the gradual gathering of like-minded friends and a bit more technology, together with the names of all the resorts, in three countries, privileged to have received our custom.

The Skier of the Week prize was followed by that of the Wimp of the Week award. Previous winners included Pam Woods. After a lunch on the slopes, she had complained that her red skis and black sticks, which she *knew* she had left propped up in a certain place, were lost. Much searching revealed her grey skis and white sticks leaning against a rail in a nearby but totally different location. Another former winner was Simon (Morgan) – much the best skier of the group, who was awarded the prize for taking two quite unnecessary private lessons and for not teaching his mother to turn somersaults on skis.

In 2004, another prize-winner was added to the roll of honour. 'Far from fighting off fierce competition for this award,' the citation says, 'the winner proved himself worthy from the first moments of the holiday. Picture the scene,' it goes on, 'all members of the Zimmerai, save one, gather at the check-in desk two hours before take-off as directed. All check in except for the worried Chairmen who wait with the last tickets, their nails bitten to the quick with anxiety, until two minutes before the flight is declared closed. This individual then saunters up, cool and suave, declaring that he could have slid round the barrier anyway, however late, due to "knowing his way about".' Ex-BA Captain Val Harder, 007 in person, won the Wimp award hands down, adding a bar to this later by landing upside down in at least two snow drifts, and, like a stranded shark, having to be ignominiously extracted from protective netting.

In a review of the week, Pip and Al gave a spirited rendition of a ditty they had tossed up, during which they announced that, with great regret, they had decided to retire from the co-chairmanship of the Order, and, even, from skiing. It was noted that 'blue balls' featured in the jingle, colourful articles apparently acquired by Pip following an unscheduled meeting with an out-of-control lady on a green run and these, which were not on display to the meeting, may have contributed to an uncomfortable feeling that a sell-by date was, sadly, approaching.

Following this, the Secretary expressed the sorrowful

feelings of the gathering. "Without," she declared, "their distinguished, nay, some might say, eccentric leadership, the Order would never have existed. Across Europe we have left a trail of ski resorts, none of which are likely to forget our passing – a passing which could possibly, with only the smallest amount of exaggeration, be compared with the ravages of the Black Death in the fourteenth century, though mercifully with a marginally lower rate of mortality."

To mark this sad occasion she presented a pair of large gold (chocolate) medals, in recognition of "wise and meritorious service, your gusto for life and laughter, your proficiency at the cribbage table and your skiing ability. This last has been an encouragement, an example and a warning to us all." Two glass bowls with candles were also awarded which were to be lit, annually and ritually, in the skiing season, for a week at a time, possibly accompanied by ceremonial *glühwein*.

Al read out a 'Notification of Compulsory Enlistment' which he alleged he had received from one A. Blair Esq. This included a list of the necessary equipment to be acquired, including an OS 1:25000 Outdoor Leisure Map of Iraq, desert boots, high factor sun cream and a one-way ticket to Riyadh. Since training time was limited, he was advised to hire videos of war films such as *The Guns of Navarone*, *Saving Private Ryan*, *Henry V*, *The Sound of Music* etc, to try to pick up a few ideas. If none of these were obtainable, 'any old John Wayne rubbish would have to do'.

'Hands then to dance and skylark, as they say in the Navy, and so to bed.'

After this the Zimmerai plodded on for another year or two but the zing had departed with Al and Pip and it became only a bare shadow of its former glory. How fortunate to have been part of it for most of its laughing, rollicking and skylarking heyday.

35

Memar

Sue Maun is a fellow naval widow living in Petersfield who has shared many a journey to out-of the-way places in the world with me. In November 1997 she and I chose Ethiopia, with its three-thousand years of independence, as a suitably mysterious and less travelled destination, and we explored the Rift valley to the south of Addis Ababa. Bird-inhabited lakes, beautiful countryside, friendly people, atrocious roads and rain for most of the time (even though the rainy season was meant to be over) greeted us. In spite of the last two drawbacks, so taken were we with the country, that in 2002 we decided to go there again. We would join an organised group and explore the 'historic' rural area in the north of the country with its mountains, rock-hewn churches and 'stellae'. I will write about these particular adventures in another volume. Here, briefly, is how I met Memar, a lad of twelve at the time, who became a distant but an important part of my life as I became in his.

From Addis Ababa (or "Adab, as we say in the trade," explained our rather appalling group leader, Graham, tossing back his long hair and jingling his bracelets) we flew up to Barhir Dar, a town on the southern shores of the vast Lake Tana. This lake is the main source of the Blue Nile which circles hugely round to the south and then to the west through a vast gorge in the Ethiopian Mountains and joins the White Nile at Khartoum in the Sudan, taking with it enormous amounts of precious silt and contributing ninety per cent of the Nile's water as it reaches Egypt.

The lake is so immense that a ferry takes two days from Bahir Dar in the south to the far north shore, stopping off for the night in a lake-side village on the way. We took a shorter trip of an hour or so to what is referred to as an island but is in fact a peninsular stretching out into the lake, named Zegie. Our boat was the *African Queen* and a flight of terns followed us, darting into the churned-up wake to grab small fish. Long skeins of geese flew past against the duck-egg blue sky.

"You will find," warned Graham, "that many children will wish to accompany you to the Church at the top of the hill and that their elders will attempt to sell you things. Don't get involved."

Two boys attached themselves to me as I climbed up the hill and at first I tried to follow the instructions by ignoring them but they were so polite and delightful that it was impossible not to chat.

They waited outside as we all visited the square fourteenth century church, the inside walls of which were covered with crude frescos of devils, saints, dragons, torture, beheadings and mythical stories. Lurid torments of the martyrs were depicted in vivid detail, with heads and limbs rolling in pools of gore as they were parted from the faithful. Everyone portrayed had large eyes – the 'goodies' showing both of these, the 'baddies' in profile. Dozens of angels' heads covered the ceiling. After a lengthy session viewing the terrors of Hell and the doubtful blessings of Heaven as depicted on the walls, I was reunited with my escorts as we walked back down the hill.

I noticed Graham was also being accompanied by a

couple of boy attendants. "Do what I say, not what I do?" I enquired innocently as I passed them.

As I walk faster than most, 'my' boys and I outstripped the rest of the group and had excellent chats on the way down. Memar was twelve and his charming small brother, Santyanu, was six. It was to be a momentous day for Memar and it changed his life and, potentially, those of his siblings.

(On a third visit to Ethiopia and this same church in 2005, I learnt that their mother had died when Memar was only eleven and their father had abandoned his four children, had married again and started another family. Memar, Santyanu, a second brother and an older sister, had been taken in by their uncle and aunt and brought up in the direst hardship. We saw something of this when the aunt invited us into their hut where, squatting on the dirt floor scattered with dried banana leaves and fanning a tiny brazier, she prepared a coffee ceremony. Hard earth benches round the walls were the only furniture. I have, fortunately, rarely seen such poverty and the absence of any comfort. We were all much moved and thanked the aunt profusely for her generous hospitality.)

I photographed the boys and with a letter accompanying the promised photographs, I asked Memar how I could help. He replied that money for his schooling was what he most needed.

At first I sent dollar bills monthly, in an envelope for which he had to sign at a post office. This worked well until one Christmas when I had sent a little extra and it failed to arrive.

Technology had surged forward, Memar had flowed with it and it became possible to communicate by email via his school, and to send money safely, once a year, from my bank to his. His aim, as with a great many other young Ethiopians, was to become a doctor – a dream well beyond any possibility of fulfilment in most cases. There are no grants or other financial backings there for a university medical course.

Memar's first year as a medical student was a disaster. He was allocated a place at the University of Dire-Dawa, a dump of a town far to the east of the country and from his home, which was built originally as a stop on the railway line from Djibouti on the coast to Addis Ababa. (This railway, the only one in Ethiopia, was immortalised by Evelyn Waugh in his book, *Scoop*.)

A further problem during this year, which in the end became a piece of good fortune for Memar, was appendicitis. This meant that he had to return home and have an operation. Recovering, he was reallocated to Bahir Dar University – much nearer to his family. He began achieving reasonable grades in his exams and I have promised to sponsor him until he qualifies and that my family will take up this obligation should I be unable to.

35

Tribal Gatherings

"I'm afraid you're too young, Simon, you're only eight. Sorry, but no-one under eleven can join," said Barney sympathetically to his boot-faced nephew. He went on preparing a rope bridge across a river. "So, Tim and David, Nick, Mark, Nutty and Charlotte, get ready to be off early tomorrow." Charlotte, pink with pleasure at squeezing into the team, was just eleven. Simon was downcast and inclined to be bolshy. "It's not fair!" he grumbled. He has held this opinion all his life so far, because that was the last of that series of Cousins' Camps and by the time he was eleven, they didn't exist, Barney having by that time moved on to more serious work.

We were camping at Gilwern, high in a Welsh field belonging to a cousin of my father. Well below us, the Heads of the Valleys road wound its way through the coalfields of South Wales. Behind us loomed the Black Mountains into which the children, in pairs, were dropped with food, maps and compasses. "Now, find your way back to Gilwern," they were instructed. Weary but triumphant, eventually they all straggled in and ate enormous meals before climbing, unwashed, into sleeping bags.

Another day they abseiled down cliffs on the Gower

coast, watched by a gathering throng on the beach. Never one to miss an opportunity, Charlotte took off her woolly hat and passed it round the crowd, harvesting a small but satisfactory sum, useful for a few bracing ice creams.

Interestingly, the Cousins' Camps have been revived in the next generation, far too late for Simon but perfect for his twins. Nick and Bids host them in Devon in the grounds of Bedford House near Tavistock in Dartmoor National Park. The age limit has been lowered and Simon has to be content to enjoy them through Anna and Jack, then nine years old, who are eager participants. Even eight-year-old Lizzie, known variously as Fizzy Lizzie or Busy Lizzie, Victoria's youngest, climbs impossible rocks, firmly harnessed to ropes and urged on by her brother, George, and four or five older cousins. Treasure hunts lure them onto Dartmoor; they paddle in canoes down the river Tamar and stare up at Isambard Kingdom Brunel's wonderful bridge. They swim in the river Walkham which borders Nick and Bids' garden, and talk far into the nights in their tents.

"Whoever goes to sleep first will be my best friend tomorrow," proclaimed Abby the eldest cousin, fatigue at last inspiring an idea brilliant enough to cause almost instant silence. Everyone wanted to be Abby's best friend. Even Jack (about whom his teacher remarked that "You can always tell where Jack is from the noise") was heard to shush someone who was bold enough to speak, with "Please be quiet, I'm trying to go to sleep."

The Family is an important and supportive idea in our clan. When small birds fly about in the garden, I am reminded of their somewhat larger and exceedingly distant relatives, the Pterosaurs. In much the same way, I am conscious of the threads that bind us together as a family, leading like a loose but unbreakable cord from the lineage of our ancestors and into the future through our descendants. It's called, unromantically, DNA. There is a great deal more to it than that.

After the death of our mother in 1988, my siblings and our spouses resolved to organise family gatherings annually. Many of these are held in Marlborough at Barney and Rachel's house, Thornsend, which, having sheltered four young Rosedales from babyhood through teens to adulthood, is always full of their many friends. These come and go freely, talk into the night, laugh, play music, eat huge meals and now bring the next generation of infant Rosedales to see their grandparents.

Not everyone, of course, can come every year to the 'Fam Gaths'. Other locations have ranged from Tim Casswell's house in the back of beyond in Wales, a Youth Hostel near Hay-on-Wye, another hostel on Dartmoor, Nick's ten acres just south of Tavistock, the Palace at Blenheim, Charlotte's house, Cley Hall in Norfolk, Noddswood before I moved and Pyramids in South Harting (when it rained rather a lot) and Victoria Casswell's house near Lutterworth in Leicestershire.

A party of about forty gathered in Devon in August 2011. Tents of all sizes decorated the field. A Cousins' Camp removed some of the older children for two or three days to an isolated bunk-house with no electricity or running water in a remote part of Dartmoor's wilderness. The youngsters will remember, for a long time, the fun of abseiling, surfing, map reading, cooking their own food, sleeping in three layers on creaky bunk-beds – and the rain.

There were a great many entirely delicious babies and young children, one of whom was lying sleepily on her grandfather Tim's chest as he and I sat chatting. "You were very quiet while I was talking to Steph," he remarked to her.

"I thought you were talking to the Queen," she murmured drowsily.

Alfie the dog had a splendid time, kindly clearing up any

food that dropped from the rich man's, or small child's, table. The evening barbecue was a fruitful source of nourishment for him as parts of delicious pork sausages (made from pigs grown in Nick's field) fell like manna from above, or the occasional doughnut escaped, or was even gently removed, from an unwary hand.

Alfie is keen (though discouraged) on pre-washing any plates as they go into the dishwasher. On this occasion he was rather too enthusiastic, placing a heavy foot on the flat open door of the washer and was horribly surprised when the entire bottom tray left its moorings and clattered explosively onto the floor, spreading unwashed bowls, plates and mugs in every direction. Suddenly, Alfie was nowhere to be found. He had fled the scene.

A great many, rather more nuclear-family Christmases (Maizels and Morgans with, often, some other relations and friends) have been spent in Cley Hall, a spacious enough house to accommodate sixteen bodies comfortably in beds with several more dotted about on mattresses. A huge Christmas tree takes over the hall, decorated by Anna and Jack with increasing skill as they grow older, with lights and baubles and tinsel.

They arrived for their first Christmas in Cley when they were about twenty months old. The two small persons tottered unsteadily from the car into the hall, Anna dressed in a rabbit suit with one pink ear up and the other down. Jack, with eyes only for the sparklingly lit tree, was a blue furry animal.

On Christmas Day when they were eight, we all went to the nearby church at Wiveton for the annual Nativity Play. There is a view from there across the marshes which have, through the centuries, replaced a navigable waterway, though a meandering small river still reminds the present age of long-vanished shipping.

As we entered the fast-filling church a woman asked them, "Would you like to take part in the play?"

She was surrounded with home-made tinsel halos, white nighties in all sizes, some sacking and an air of authority. Before she knew it, Anna had been transformed into a particularly delicious angel and Jack into a shepherd boy. Anna was instructed to join the angelic choir near the altar and Jack sat down in the chancel with the other scruffy little shepherds who were giggling and making faces at their parents.

A powerful lady mounted the pulpit and took charge above the social chat. The silence was instant. Adults were to stay seated throughout the play, she boomed. Any children too small to join the cast could stand on the pews as they wished. Everyone was to gather for the procession when instructed.

The principal characters, Mary, the Archangel Gabriel and Herod the King, had clearly had a few rehearsals but probably not quite enough. The first two got through the Annunciation perfectly but there followed several sparkling intrusions of real life into the well-known story. An almost impossibly small cherub, already crumpled and with her halo long since abandoned, broke away from the heavenly host and rushed down the aisle. "Must have a pee," we heard her mutter as she whizzed past.

The little shepherds shivered in their field by night, sheep bells indicating their flock. Rubbing their eyes and throwing up their hands in surprise, they gave a convincing show of being astonished by the appearance of the angels. These ranged in size from cherub to archangel and were perched rather precariously on the altar which stood in for the heavens on high. They announced the baby's arrival.

The Wise Men wandered down the aisle, asking where the new King could be found, one of them fiddling with a mobile phone. Herod, in real life the proprietor of the local garden centre, in a scarlet robe and a gold paper crown, mounted his pew and shouted loudly in protest at the rumoured prospect of a rival monarch. He was booed and hissed by one and all. Unfortunately, he now forgot his lines and had to be prompted by his son. "Tell them go home via Jerusalem," the boy whispered loudly.

The angels now set off for Bethlehem followed by a mêlée of shepherds and kings, unfortunately down the wrong aisle.

The stentorian voice thundered out above the triumphant organ.

"Angels, you are going in the wrong direction. Please come back and go down the right-hand aisle."

With some difficulty, the angels threaded their way back through the shepherds and, following a wobbly star on a stick, managed to find the correct approach.

We all sang our way to the west end, to the vestry which was standing in for a stable, where a real baby was enjoying a bottle, held by her real mother and attended by her real father.

The finale, with a tableau of all the characters grouped before the altar, was flash-lit by adoring, camera-wielding parents, causing 'Jesus' to utter cries of protest and having to be removed.

We trooped out into the biting-cold north Norfolk wind, warmed and happy, with an ex-shepherd boy and an ex-angel hopping excitedly over the frozen grass, along the tiny road bordering the frosty marshes and over the ancient humpback bridge, drawn by the imminent prospect of presents and turkey.

36

Geoffrey

During my married life I had come to know most of David's large extended family. Having no first cousins of my own, I could see how enviable and important these relations were and what my siblings and I had missed. Geoffrey was the one we saw most often since he and his wife Hersey farmed near Salisbury and we would take the children there to play with his children, Bridget and David, on the farm when we were stationed near enough.

He was the youngest son of Uncle Ed, the Bishop, first of Southampton and later of Truro. Born in 1920, Geoffrey was six months younger than David. He had left Oxford after graduating in geography and, like my father, had joined the Colonial Service and travelled to Nigeria as the war began. Joining the Army out there he trained, and later somewhat incongruously led, a party of Nigerians to fight the Japanese in Burma, the black man fighting the yellow man led by a white man. He was seriously wounded but had survived, somewhat battered, to take up farming and marry Hersey.

"It's extraordinarily lucky that I lost an eye and they counted it as a limb," Geoffrey remarked. He wore a piratical black eye-patch. "The compensation from the British Limbless Ex-Servicemen's Association kept my farming head just above the poverty line till things looked up."

On seeing him, small boys tugged excitedly at their mothers' arms. "Look, Mum," they whispered loudly, "there's a pirate."

"I'm a retired pirate," Geoffrey would reassure them, "and I don't sail under the Jolly Roger any longer."

His two elder brothers, Hugh and Robert were killed in the war. Hersey's widowed elder sister, Pamela, had been married to Robert. When he was killed she was left with a very small daughter, Jane, and a son, Hugh, who was born nine days after his father's death in 1943. In 1948, two years before I met David, I had encountered them when they were living in the Close in Winchester with Uncle Ed and Aunt Blue. I had not then met Geoffrey.

For many years, Hersey was a good helpmate on the farm and a loving mother to their children. However, she began to develop dementia and the farm had to go. He cared selflessly for her, coping with the long years of strain by maintaining the vigorous and flourishing sense of humour inherited by most Morgans.

"I can't come to the door," he once shouted in answer to the bell. "I'm washing a naked woman in the bathroom."

In 1998, seven years after the deaths of our respective spouses, Geoffrey and I threw in our lot together. After David's death I had carried on the tradition of meeting for lunch once a month with two other Morgan cousins' widows, Dick's Sylvia and John's Kay, and we agreed that cousin Geoffrey, whom we all knew well, should be invited to join us. There was no rush about this romance; we just gravitated, quite gently, into attraction and into enjoying each other's company and, finally, into love.

He came to live in Harting and was with me for six years. "When I love someone, it's for ever," he said to me. My friends gathered him to their hearts. What is so good about joining up with a close member of the family is that there is no need to explain who one is talking about; for instance, Aunt Kit and her Kitticisms are, of course, a common, tribal, humorous memory.

When I opened Pyramids garden as usual under the National Gardens Scheme one summer soon after his arrival, I overheard one of the visitors asking "Who is that charming old gentleman?"

He raised a quizzical eyebrow. "Old?" he queried. Had he not avoided being born on twenty-ninth of February 1920 by arriving one day earlier (or at least his father had registered his birth as the twenty-eighth) he might have been able to remark that he had had only twenty-one birthdays. Who can tell what birthday-party difficulties this difference of a day circumvented – like those of Frederick in *The Pirates of Penzance*?

Geoffrey won the first prize in a raffle at a village hall occasion one year, and was fast making for a box of chocolates when I managed to divert him into choosing a far more exciting award. This was for a car and four people to cross the Channel to France, free. We gathered together a pair of other senior citizens, my friends Grace Tyson and Catalina Aykroyd, crossed the sea and arrived in Cherbourg. This turned out to be a good deal further from St Malo, our destination, than I had expected. I insisted on driving, due to my suspicion that the others were well past their sell-by date for manoeuvring on the wrong side of the road in France.

The town of St Malo has stout walls and a one-way system of navigation. After we had roundly negotiated this several times in an effort to locate our hotel in the dark, a great many unsolicited instructions came floating over from the back seats.

"I'm sure we've passed that gate more than once," was one helpful comment.

"You *must* stick to the walls, it's the only way we'll ever find it," was another useful suggestion.

I lost my cool. "I'm *sticking* to the bloody walls," I uttered rudely, as exasperation and exhaustion caught up with me. A shocked silence ensued. "Sorry," I mumbled. "It must be here somewhere." One more nervous circumambulation and there was the hotel, passed several times already but not recognised. We squeezed into the world's smallest lift and were borne on high, gratefully, to our rooms.

The outing was much more fun than a box of chocolates, even with that unpromising start. We ate splendidly, we toured about, we explored ancient St Malo and its colourful harbour and I have a watercolour painting of nearby Dinard, presented on our return by my grateful, and probably relieved, passengers, as a memento of the adventure.

My friend Grace and he played Scrabble. This was no casual time-passing game. The competition was intense. "My Enemy", Grace called him affectionately when he won, though there was a certain amount of finger-tapping if he took too long thinking out his next wily move.

He was a stimulating companion, much given to questioning my often ill thought-out theories and pronouncements. "What, exactly, do you mean by that?" was a frequent, disconcerting question. What *had* I meant by that? I was forced to collect my thoughts into a more coherent stream of consciousness.

We continued regularly to visit Sylvia, cousin Dick's widow. She was ensconced in a Nursing Home in Winchester from which we often scooped her out to a pub lunch in her wheelchair.

"Do you know what I'd like to do?" she asked on one occasion. "No," we said cautiously – as well we might.

"I'd love to go to Paris once more," she declared.

I am not one to resist a challenge. "Why not?" I said, ignoring Geoffrey's look of horror. "We'll go."

The Nursing Home acquiesced in an idiosyncratic way. Together with huge packets of Inco pads, they packed three evening dresses, presumably to provide a choice for our two wild and sophisticated nights in Paris, and only one, hopelessly inadequate, night dress.

We travelled first class by Eurostar. Well in advance, I had organised a helper to meet us at Waterloo and put us on to the train. On our arrival, in good time, there was no such person. We hurried the length of the station but because of the wheelchair we were not allowed through to the train till the helper arrived. Eventually, with Geoffrey's coat flying, Sylvia driven as if by Jehu and luggage whirling along behind, we reached our coach. Clambering in, we sat down, breathless. Immediately, the train moved smoothly off. It waits for no man.

"I am surprised to see that no sea water is coming through the roof," remarked Sylvia, tongue in cheek. We toyed with our glasses of (included-in-the-price) wine as we dipped into the tunnel.

The taxi drive to the small Hotel Suede, in *Arrondissement Septième*, where I had stayed before with my friend Catalina, was delayed by demonstrations *en route* and cost an enormous fare. In the evening, we sauntered down the road to a tiny restaurant, almost full of locals, and managed to squeeze the wheelchair into the smallest possible space.

We hired a car with a driver for the whole of the next day and 'did' Paris. At the foot of the Eiffel Tower there is a flight of steps to the bottom level up which Sylvia said she would like to go. With what felt like the amount of effort needed to raise London's Tower Bridge, we reached the top of the steps and, breathlessly, admired the view. Getting down again brought us close to calamity. Several well-wishing locals sprang forward to help, grasping the wheelchair by its arms – which then came away in their surprised hands. This left Sylvia suspended over the brink of disaster and me hanging on to the chair, every muscle braced against catastrophe.

We recovered our nerves over lunch in a café near the Louvre chosen by our driver. Further excitements were fortunately avoided as we drove slowly past Sylvia's long-remembered and much exclaimed-at sights.

"Oh, Montmartre!" she cried. "Dick and I came here together. How lovely!" and "There's Notre Dame – always so dark inside – and the river! – oh, I am enjoying this."

Our return journey, during which we found ourselves at Waterloo in the rush hour, was also verging on the memorable. Sylvia in her chair had to be parked in a sort of guard's van together with bicycles, parcels, a couple of dogs and an empty pram, the erstwhile occupant of which had been borne away by its mother to a more salubrious part of the train. On seeing us all emerge from Winchester station, the first taxi driver in the queue for passengers drove off, eager not to have to cope with awkward customers. We saved the passenger seat of the next taxi from a certain dampness (we had, after all, been a long way from Inco pad-changing facilities for some hours) by placing a copy of the newspaper, *Le Figaro,* in a strategic position.

The Nursing Home received a moist but delighted and grateful Sylvia back into their care. Geoffrey and I went home where I slept for the next fourteen hours without moving.

In the summer of 2004, Geoffrey became ill. He was admitted at first to Haslar, the former naval hospital in Gosport, a brilliant place staffed by Service doctors and nurses but an arduous drive away from Harting. Transferred to Queen Alexandra's, north of Portsmouth – nearer for visiting but not quite in the same class as Haslar – he deteriorated. I scooped him out and he was at home for a few days. My nurse-friend Tessa tended him lovingly. On his last day, he suddenly sat up and looked out of his window at the wonderful view of the Downs.

"How beautiful!" he said and died early the next morning in August 2004.

37

Taking Leave of God

Being by nature good, wise and witty, Geoffrey had no need of a supernatural personality to urge him to keep his integrity intact. But, "It's no good getting rid of God," he insisted, (though he had) "if you don't put something in his, her or its place." Endless enjoyable discussions followed, about what the enigmatic 'something' might be, but this ethical mystery remained, of course, unsolved. For several centuries, intellectuals and philosophers have been pondering the question. Geoffrey and I were unlikely to do better.

It was when Diana was ill and after she died that I became disillusioned with organised religion. I had been, in the Eighties, the Churchwarden of Harting Church for eight years. Gradually, I found that it was impossible for me to say the Creed with integrity, since however much I busily interpreted the words as 'true-for-people-when-it-was-written-sixteen-hundred-years-ago', I no longer believed it. Going to Church and thus appearing to others to acquiesce in the dogmas felt hypocritical. I stopped going. No-one asked me why, not even the rector whose Churchwarden I had been.

The thoughtful and reflective retired Bishop of Edinburgh, Richard Holloway, has also given up on a supernatural God. In his book, *Looking in the Distance*, he writes:

The universe is no longer cosy, no longer exclusively organised for our protection and welfare. We may not be ready for it but we are on our own; we have broken away, made the separation. The other side of that frightening thought is that this is the way it has always really been, though we could never admit it to ourselves. There is no-one but us.

And again:

The world is all before us, with its promise and threat, and we will make of it what we will... Ready or not, we have come of age and are now responsible for what we make of ourselves. The thought may frighten us or it may exhilarate us... We have lost the protection of the old certainties, it's true, but it's also quite liberating to be responsible for ourselves at last... Maybe the central lesson, that we should try to care for one another, has stuck.

In other words, 'Love thy neighbour as thyself.'

We human beings, with our relatively large brains and intelligence, have to take human responsibility for our own lives, our families, our communities, the environment and people who need our help – there is no-one else. By becoming adult like this, we are giving up the undoubted comfort of dependence and unthinking obedience to a God we have ourselves created but this in no way diminishes one's sense of delight in the natural world nor one's search for meaning in one's life.

I read a book called *God in Us* by Anthony Freeman – a vicar who was dismissed from his Sussex parish by the Bishop of Chichester for what were considered his subversive views on the existence of God. I found it a breath of fresh air.

I joined the Sea of Faith network. (This is misnamed in my opinion. The title derives from the poem *Dover Beach* by Matthew Arnold who heard the 'grating' of dragged pebbles with its 'melancholy, long, withdrawing roar'... leaving us 'here, as on a darkling plain'... with 'confused alarms... where ignorant armies clash by night'. This is hardly an apt name for a network of intelligent and hopeful people who have, on the whole, given up on a supernatural God.)

In fact, it is a network that connects people from all walks of life, including a great many clergy, who consider that all religions, from that of the earliest cave-dwellers with their fear of inexplicable phenomena such as thunder, lightning, eclipses and volcanic eruptions, to the multiple variations of faith that the human race has since devised, are *human* creations and the fruit of *human* imagination and that we created God in *our* image rather than the other way round.

Religions were invented to placate with various sacrifices the invisible beings thought to be responsible for the strange and dangerous and frightening happenings. They evolved over the millennia and became rigid with rules laid down by a powerful hierarchy and gradually developed into instruments of manipulation, authority and fear, with sets of laws from which people deviated at their peril. Christianity, possibly in particular, has a fearful history of bigotry, torture, religious warfare and the denial of scientific advances. That the improved status of women in the Church should still be a source of extreme division in the twenty-first century is indicative of closed minds stiffened by prejudice and a clinging to ancient rules. So is the intolerance of homosexuality among some parts of the world-wide Church.

Christianity, it has to be said, has, at the same time, also shaped our world and our culture; its dogmas and disciplines, morals and creeds, have given shape and comfort to very many lives. For centuries it has inspired wonderful architecture, music, paintings and literature. And the example and many of the teachings of Jesus can be followed fruitfully when attempting to lead a decent human life.

The word 'God' for me is a metaphor for those values, generated by human culture, which can be thought of as ultimate and eternal. Blake called them 'mercy, pity, peace and love', but the Quaker, David Boulton, in his booklet, *A Reasonable Faith*, adds 'justice, truth, compassion, integrity and beauty' to this list.

I do not find any difference in the loving, generous, compassionate and hospitable behaviour of those of my friends who still go regularly to Church and believe, those who still go but don't believe and those who do neither. I hope my own conduct hasn't changed for the worse since my rational brain took over, somewhat painfully, from my religious upbringing. And I can still feel a sense of wonder at the glorious splendour of Nature without there having to be a supernatural creator.

I was not aware of myself before I was born (and how incredibly fortunate we are to be alive given the many hazards during the last several million years which might have prevented our existence and survival as unique human beings) nor will I be any more concerned after my death. David Boulton, in the same book, writes that:

We are part of a process which began long before our birth and will continue long after our death. Indeed, it is precisely because every individual life makes its own unique contribution to the drama of the living universe that it is seen as having 'eternal' significance. And it is precisely because our one life in this world is [as far as we can know] all that we have that we must make the most of it. To see life 'here below' as a mere preparation for joys 'above' (or horrors in outer darkness) is to diminish, to trivialise it.'

For those who are left, whom I knew and loved in my life and who loved me, there will be some happy memories. These, together with my much loved children and grandchildren, will, I believe, constitute most of what I can hope for that amounts to immortality.

38

Rupert

Just after Christmas, 2009, a most terrible and shocking tragedy befell the family. Barney and Rachel's eldest son, Rupert, who was the Outdoor Activities master at Marlborough College, was killed by an avalanche on Ben Nevis. He was thirty-seven, married to Ulrika, with two small children. Ted was three years old and Svea just one. It was the first of two bitter winters with more snow round the country than for many years, beautiful but in some instances, deadly.

Rupert was highly qualified and fully equipped for the weather. He was in Scotland on the last leg of a further qualification to become a Mountain Guide in France. He and Ulrika had been slowly rescuing a wreck of a house in France and had planned to live and work there. He and one of his four companions on Ben Nevis were crossing a gully when the avalanche swept down, engulfing the pair. The others raised the alarm but it was not possible to rescue them.

The arrangements for his funeral were hampered by further falls of snow and the habit of the Scots of taking extra holidays over Hogmanay. When, at last, his body was able to travel south, snow again made for difficulties.

"We can't get the coffin to the church in the usual

hearse," said the undertaker. "It would never get up the hill. We'll have to use a four-wheel-drive pickup-truck."

Covered in flowers, this truck was felt to be heart-warmingly right for Rupert. After the service, we stood in the snow, smiles and hugs hiding the sorest of spirits, as he was borne away. Ted and Svea were taken to the private cremation a day or so later.

The Chapel in Marlborough College is said to hold a thousand people. It was completely full for Rupert's Memorial Service – and the more junior members of the school were, in addition, gathered in the adjacent Hall with a video link. It was clear from the testaments that he had been a most inspiring and encouraging teacher and climbing companion, drawing people out to achieve feats they were sure they couldn't do – but found, with his help, that they could. One pupil, Head Boy of Turner House, spoke of the affection in which the boys in that particular house had held Rupert. He would play football with them – "though he wasn't much good at the game, and on one occasion a boy preparing to shoot a goal was surprised to see the goalie, Mr Rosedale, upside down, hanging by his feet from the crossbar."

Around five hundred letters or cards sent to Barney and Rachel testified to the love and warmth he had inspired amongst his friends, the friends of his parents, the staff at the school and the countless pupils he had encouraged and motivated.

It is unimaginably sad for Barney and Rachel, his siblings and Ulrika, and indeed for all of us, but also, of course, for Ted and Svea who, as they grow up, will hardly be able to remember their father. His memory will be kept bright for them by all the family.

A Scots pine has been planted high on a hillside, overlooking a most glorious Wiltshire view, as a memorial to Rupert. The children love decorating it with coloured ribbons as well as climbing on a nearby conveniently fallen beech. Barney, Rachel and I walked there on a beautiful spring day, cool and sunny, a year and a few months after his death. If *I* found it difficult to keep the tears away, I can only imagine what it must be like for his mother and father. To lose an adult child – brought into the world, nurtured, loved; to have watched with pride as he grew into an exceptional man – this must be one of the saddest events that life can throw at anyone. And yet people survive, albeit in a changed world which, though filled with happy memories, still has a Rupert-shaped space impossible to fill.

39

The Isles of Scilly

It was Barney and Rachel who 'discovered' St Martin's. It must have been in the mid-Eighties that they first visited the island with their children, followed swiftly by Nick and Bids with their four-year-old Caroline and the infant Christopher.

I first joined them in 1989. After a day of ominous premonitions of disaster which gave those Morgans who are prone to pessimism even at the best of times, cause to be even gloomier than usual and to question whether the holiday was a viable proposition at all. Christopher had been sick on and off all the previous day, even without the excuse of a sea-crossing. An official gale-force wind and monsoon rains in a manner vividly remembered from our time in Singapore had lashed the country all that evening. David, who rather wisely had decided not to accompany us, phoned during the storm with a detectable note of satisfaction in his voice at his decision.

At midnight Chris reopened negotiations with his stomach and threw up *in* his sleep *in* his bed, causing his parents serious loss of sleep. In spite of this, a take-off of exemplary smoothness was achieved at 5.45 am, both cars crawling on their knees with accumulated freight and bodies.

Cornwall basked in a beautifully clear but windy early

morning. On reaching Penzance from Plymouth, we were faced with a notice at the foot of the *Scillonian's* gangway. This read 'VERY ROUGH CROSSING. Intending passengers are advised NOT TO TRAVEL.'

In spite of this morale-quenching information, we and several score of other intrepid folk (some, bravely if foolishly, with day return tickets) boarded the boat and we settled ourselves in the sun and the lee of a useful bulkhead. We set off into the teeth of what felt like a full-blown gale.

"Not at all," said Nick, "we'll be in the shelter of the land for some time yet."

The sea was impressively exciting, with large waves on top of which the *Scillonian* appeared to pause briefly before dropping off suddenly into the holes behind, the accompanying rolling from side to side adding to the unease of one's internal arrangements. It was with some relief that we disembarked, most of us a delicate shade of green, into the sun on St Mary's quay.

Life immediately began to slow down to the unhurried pace of the Islands. We crossed to St Martin's where Barney and Rachel and their friends Jan and Don Patterson (previous medical colleagues in Nepal and whom I had met there) had arrived a few days earlier. They and their assorted children were already ensconced in well-pitched tents. They all looked full of health, energy and bounce in rather sharp contrast to us new arrivals after our early start and the sea-tossed voyage.

The camp-site is protected from the sea and some winds by bracken-covered dunes, threaded with small paths leading to the sandy beach with its line of colourful boats drawn up safely above the tide line.

From the beach, all but one of the five inhabited islands can be seen, flung, as it were, like a necklace, round a lost land beneath the sea. Tresco looms with its trees to the west and

St Agnes and St Mary's, to the south. Bryher is invisible from here, hidden beyond Tresco. Hundreds of scattered smaller islands and groups of large rocks comprise the archipelago, making sailing in these waters almost too exciting. Many a large sailing ship has, through the centuries, come to grief in these seas on rocks skulking just beneath the surface of a high tide.

Wind-surfing, treasure-hunting, dinghy-sailing, mackerel-fishing, shell-seeking, swimming, kite-flying, shrimping, painting, walking or reading; all these and other activities filled up the days. On a boat trip to see the seals on the Eastern Isles, a long-running argument broke out as to whether a particular kind of sea-bird was a shag or a cormorant or, in desperation, both, but the seals took no notice and lay about plentifully on the rocks, gazing at us with their doe-like eyes.

On the north side of St Martin's is Great Bay – a long stretch of curving sand from which, on a clear day, the far off ghost of Land's End lurks. If there are more than two or three little gatherings of families on the beach, the cry goes up, "My *dear*, the *crowds*."

The red and white striped Day Mark on the northern headland, built in the seventeenth century, becomes the 'there-and-back' target for the annual St Martin's race. A walk right round the island takes a mere hour or so – longer if there is a stop at Toby's bakery for essential nourishment.

Long before the Rosedales discovered their favourite island, Uncle Ed Morgan, then Bishop of Truro, had holidayed there as locum for the local vicar. So Geoffrey, Hersey, Pamela and other Morgans had also been there before us – a further link between the families.

Much longer before that, my great-great-grandfather, John Henry Pelly, had overseen the plans, as an Elder Brother of Trinity House, of the building of the second Bishop Rock Lighthouse, in 1852. (The first attempt had ended in disaster. It was swept away, before completion, in 1850.) The first stone of the new one was laid in 1852, just before John Henry's death and it was completed and lit in 1857. Some thirty years later the Lighthouse was strengthened and heightened to fifty-one metres. As the tallest and best-known tower in the British Isles, it keeps a sea-battered watch over some particularly jagged rocks.

Simon and Sally, before the advent of the twins, came one summer for the first time. Being in the airline world, they had taken advantage of cheaper flights for staff to fly, as they hoped, all the way to Penzance. At Exeter two full-fare-paying passengers turned up, inconsiderately. Simon and Sally were turned off the small plane. With difficulty they made their way to Exeter station and caught a train. Half way to Penzance, it made an unscheduled stop and failed to start again. "This 'ere train's no good," announced the guard. "All passengers get off 'ere and there may be another train before long."

Slowly they crawled to Penzance, far too late to catch the *Scillonian*, and the last planes had long since been parked for the night. It was before the era of mobile phones so we, huddling out of the rain in the largest of the tents in St Martin's, had no idea what had happened to them – they just didn't appear. About noon the next day – it was still raining and we were still huddling – the tent flap opened and two extremely soggy people, looking as if they'd been standing under a waterfall, dripped into the tent. It was not a good first experience for them of the glories of the Islands.

The second time they were persuaded to join us was even more dramatic. A mighty storm, coming from the wrong direction, ie the east, swept over the islands and the camp-site, shredding tents and causing swamps. Babies and small children were caught up and carried to safety, the few empty rooms in guest houses were immediately snapped up and locals kindly sheltered the worst saturated and buffeted victims.

The children – Chris, James and Lucy – and I, like drowning rats abandoning a submerging ship, were lucky enough to find one empty guest-house room into which we all squashed. Back in the camp-site, the able-bodied did their best to alleviate the plight of the wet, the wind-blown and the tentless, and had a lovely time afterwards in the only pub, the Seven Stones.

This gives completely the wrong idea of the islands. They are beautiful, remote and friendly, often sunny and sometimes windless, and surrounded by the clearest possible bluish-green sea which is horribly chilly in spite of the Gulf Stream. It is far too cold for swimming though some of my relations do so in the early morning and return shivering and blue for breakfast, saying, through chattering teeth, how lovely it was.

Strange to relate, Simon and Sally have not returned to the island – nor in fact have they been invited, since they are clearly doom-laden, weather-wise. "Couldn't you at least lend us Anna and Jack?" we ask annually. But they live almost into Kent and it's far easier and cheaper to go east to France for a holiday than to cross the width of southern England.

40

Hobbies

For some twenty years, as I open a new Dodo Pad diary in January, I make a resolution. "I will not deface this elegant and spotless purity with aimless doodles," I promise myself. Every year this resolution fades away within a week. No-one else could possibly discern my engagements, hidden as they are behind small pictures and patterns, with every crossed line turned into a sparkling star and every drawn face shaded. In the days when the whole family's activities had to be recorded, the five columns served us all well. Dad, Mum, Nick, Charlotte and Simon headed the weekly columns and it could be seen at a glance where potential clashes of interest lay.

"You can't be playing tennis on Tuesday afternoon, Nick – what about your dental appointment at three? And Charlotte, I won't be able to drive you to that party on Saturday evening – I'm going to the theatre."

Now I have it all to myself and enjoy the freedom to cover every page with hieroglyphics.

I have always squiggled with a pencil. Way back in Singapore, with more leisure than has ever been possible since, I dabbled with oils. Since then, it's been watercolours. I have attended painting groups and classes, been on painting holidays to Greece and Italy, and even had an exhibition in Petersfield in 1992 at the invitation of the gallery which framed such of my pictures as seemed worthy of this.

In the year 2000, Harting produced a Millennium Map of itself, with paintings of various parts of the village. I painted about six of these and others were contributed by a range of the talented artists and designers living here. I have found that I need either to have a deadline to paint at all or to go regularly to a painting group or a class. Ordinary life in a village, with many friends and activities, with gardening and hens and family visits and dog walks and travel, intervenes all too readily to foil the aspiration to paint or, indeed, to write. Living here sometimes feels like an enjoyable full-time job.

In the autumn of 2008 I was loafing about outside Waitrose in Petersfield when I saw a notice advertising an evening-class called 'Write Now'. It was to start later that week and was organised by Sheila Dainton. (By chance, it turned out that she was already a friend of my great friend, Sue Jones whom she had met on a train journey.) "I'm going to join that," I declared to myself, and discovered that there was one place left on the course. It was tutored by a distinguished past editor of both *The Listener* and *Readers' Digest* (among many other claims of note) Russell Twisk – who lives in East Harting and was already a friend – and Colin Dunne, a well-known author and journalist – who became one, as did Sheila.

The group numbered about twelve and the quality of most of the work produced was often tremendously good and hilariously funny. The aim of most of the other students was to learn the art of writing publishable articles for a variety of magazines (research, research and research) and how to present them to the editors in a professional manner. My (different) aim was to write this memoir but it was kindly tolerated and, of course, I learnt an immense amount about writing in general and was, in fact, the first student to have an article published – in *The Oldie* magazine! (Colin has a rule that only one exclamation mark is allowed per year, so that's the one for 2010. Another rule, regularly neglected by me, is that never a day should pass without two hundred and fifty words, as a minimum, being tapped out on the computer and saved for posterity.)

I don't suppose Feminism can be classed as a hobby but it has been an inclination (though not of the aggressive, bra-burning, man-hating sort) all my adult life. An advertisement appeared in a local Petersfield newspaper way back in the Seventies for a cook for a Nursing Home. The pay for a male chef, it stated, was x, that for a female to do the same job was x minus 10%. (This was before the days of the Equal Pay Act which was meant to put an end to this sort of overt discrimination, though women's pay still lags behind that of men.) I wrote a furious letter to the local newspaper asking how it was possible for an employer to show such unfairness so blatantly. Women often had as many commitments, responsibilities and dependants as men, I said; how could he justify this inequity? His answer appeared in the paper. It was perfectly legal, he wrote.

Harting Old Club is one of the oldest Friendly Societies in the land. Every year, in the middle of the Festivities, a great many men of the village leave their stall or post or barbecue, and by invitation, repair to the village hall for the Feast. The womenfolk are left to 'man' the stalls and keep the show on the road, sometimes in pouring rain. Others are actually preparing the Feast, to which no member of the female sex is ever invited.

I wrote to the Editor of the Harting Parish News, who, on reading it remarked, "Brave woman." It ran as follows:

It is a truth universally acknowledged (at least in Harting) that several dead bodies would have to be stepped over before any change in a patriarchal tradition could be contemplated.

However, I know that I am not the only person in the village who considers it an anachronism in the 21ˢᵗ century that only male members of the community are invited to the Feast at the Harting Festivities.

Other bastions of male supremacy have, however reluctantly, given up sexism in the last hundred years – the Church of England [to a certain extent], the suffrage system, the professions, the Services – and even some Gentlemen's Clubs have somewhat grudgingly acknowledged that women, too, are members of the human race.

I wonder if the time has come (preferably without any stepping over corpses) for Harting Old Club to reconsider its policy.

A meeting was called, discussion invited, a vote taken. The outcome was precisely as I expected. There was to be absolutely no change.

So much for my efforts to convert the world! Luckily it is possible in Harting to continue to be friends, with a complete lack of animosity or rancour, with people who hold diametrically opposed views.

Charlotte gave a splendid party for my eightieth birthday. I specially thanked her, Nick, Simon and others for kind words uttered, for many presents and for the wonderful food. In my reply to the toast I quoted Trotsky. He had remarked that old age is the most unexpected of all the things that can happen to a man. "Quite true," I said, "and the aphorism applies to women, too. And while we are on the subject of the sexes, I would like to quote Queen Victoria's views on these. 'The Queen,' she wrote angrily, 'is most anxious to enlist everyone who can speak or write to join in checking this mad wicked folly of Women's Rights with all its attendant horrors, on which her poor feeble sex is bent, forgetting every sense of womanly feeling and propriety. It is a subject which makes the Queen so furious that she cannot contain herself. God created men and women differently – then let them remain in their own position.' Those of you," I said, "who are acquainted with my own views will know how *very* much I agree with hers."

41

Summing Up

How does one sum up a life? Is it possible in a few words? Probably not.

Should one do so? Is writing a memoir just an ego-trip? This chronicle with all its faults, I dedicate to my descendants with a very great deal of love and the hope that those further away into the future, whom I will never know and whose lives I can only guess at, will find the same interest in it that I and my siblings found in our great-grandfather's manuscript. (I find it reassuring that he, who was convinced that it was right to forsake the religion in which he was born and brought up and to take a different path in life, should be followed much later by a great-grand-daughter, and other family members, who have taken a similar step.)

Mine has been a life full of loving relationships – and in these I include, of course, my beloved David, our three remarkable children, their spouses and their seven exceptionally special offspring, my three much loved siblings, my wider family of nephews and nieces, the very special Geoffrey and my many very close friends (who, if not named individually in my story, will know who I mean and how much they are valued).

I also include some particularly delightful dogs: Boy and

Major from my childhood, the Peke Woolley, the Spaniel Bracken and the favourite black Labrador (Morgan's) Rum. Alfie, my last and largest, a gentle chocolate giant, is not only an affectionate companion (and, like most Labradors, a dreadful food-thief) but also my personal trainer, taking me for walks even on the coldest, wettest and most dismal of days. He has his own personal best friend, Gus, a charming and sensitive Pointer in whose house, belonging to my friend, Angela Church, Alfie is as much at home as Gus is at Pyramids.

My life has been unusually well filled with the marvellous stimulation of travel to many parts of the world, with skiing and tennis into my eighties, with a variety of the most valued friendships with both men and women, with reading, with voluntary work, gardening, painting, contributing to nursing, naval and village matters, and towards the end, with discovering I could write.

Life-enhancing friends – these come, after my immediate family, probably the highest in value of all the contributory factors to human happiness. They adorn my existence like pearls and are cherished gratefully, whether I deserve them or not.

No-one's life is lived entirely on the 'sunlit uplands'. There have been the deaths of many loved people close to me, or close to people I love, both almost equally painful. There was a miscarried baby, whom I have always thought of as Paul, who arrived on my twenty-sixth birthday, far too early at twenty weeks to survive, and is not forgotten.

Wars have raged somewhere in the world for most of the twentieth century and into the twenty-first and though this is a personal memoir and not a world history, it has been impossible not to be totally aware of, indeed in some cases emotionally involved with, the major wars and more minor conflicts skirmishing through the years, many arising from clashes of different religions. Will the human race ever find a way to live in tolerance, harmony and some kind of equality with its fellow Passing Guests?

The Great Depression of the late Twenties and Thirties into which I was born, passed unnoticed over my childish head. It is disheartening and depressing, though, to note that now, eighty years or so on, we seem not to have learnt the lessons of history and to be going through some equally dire international financial shocks and disasters, wars, revolutions and cruel dictatorships. And still, a great many people of the over-populated world are poor, hungry and undereducated. Fighting and corruption continue, children are dying unnecessarily and women and girls in many countries are still oppressed and treated as the chattels of men.

For the lucky ones like me, the glass has mostly been more than 'half full'. I have suffered only my fair share of sorrows and bereavement, counterbalanced with more than my fair share of joy and love, laughter and friendship, and much less of my fair share of ill health. Wonderfully fortunate, with hardly a serious illness to my name, I have been, so far, scarcely any trouble to the NHS.

Funerals are important rites of passage for those left behind and are not for the benefit of the departed. All the same, when contemplating my leaving, I find it pleasant to visualise the place in which to lie, in a village where I have lived for half my life. I shall be totally unaware of anything, so that whatever is planned and wherever it happens is a matter only of expediency and convenience for my family and friends. Digging out weeds at the monthly Churchyard Working Parties in the summer and enjoying the company of my friends the mowers, strimmers, choppers and bonfire enthusiasts – and the half-time coffee-break – I know that Harting, with its glorious backdrop of the lofty green and wooded Downs where I have walked for years, its friendly community spirit and its beauty, is where my heart is.

I hope that any act of celebration of what has been good in my life will offer serenity and comfort to those I have loved and who have loved me – love being the only deeply important thing in this world.

The End